Tim Waltmen
1976

Man-making Words

Man-making Words

Selected poems of Nicolás Guillén
Translated, Annotated, with an
Introduction by Robert Márquez
and David Arthur McMurray

University of Massachusetts Press

A few translations included in
this anthology have
already appeared in
print. Acknowledgments
are therefore due to:
Evergreen Review for "Five Chinese
Songs," and "Sell Me?"
Monthly Review Press, publishers
of *Patria o Muerte: The
Great Zoo & Other Poems
by Nicolás Guillén,
1928-1970,* for permission
to use "My Last Name"
which along with "What
Color?" and "Sunday
Reading" also appeared in
Volume 1, Number 2 of
*Confrontation: A Journal
of Third World Literature.*

These translations are for
      Angela Davis
      Dr. Frantz Fanon
      El compañero Debray
For the people of Vietnam
And all the rest who struggle
      To give breath
      To Che's New Man,
Against "a closed society
in which life has no taste,
in which the air is tainted,
in which ideas & men are corrupt."

THE TRANSLATORS

Contents

Introduction

Give me initiative,
spermatic, prophesying
man-making words.
Ralph Waldo Emerson
Journals

Just two years younger than the century, Nicolás Guillén came of age at a time when the peoples of the world were beginning consciously to move apart, to define their positions *vis-à-vis* the struggle between progress and reaction which continues to shape contemporary history. Today, as his seventieth birthday draws near, he is the dynamic National Poet[1] of a country which has won and is consolidating an exemplary victory in that struggle.

By design, and with a great deal more consistency than many of his contemporaries, Guillén has spoken to, been formed by, the concrete human issues of both his immediate community and the larger world. But to conclude, merely for this reason, that his work as an intellectual[2] has been political is to overlook what really distinguishes it. There should be no necessity at this advanced stage in the history of criticism to repeat that the responses—Combray as well as Macchu Picchu, Clarissa Dalloway along with Bigger Thomas—of an artist are always political; and even if Guillén had followed the poetic example of his Spanish namesake, Jorge, observa-

1. The same year (1961) he was proclaimed *Poeta nacional,* Guillén became President of the Union of Cuban Writers and Artists (UNEAC), a position he still holds. He also edits *La gaceta de Cuba,* UNEAC's official cultural periodical, and serves on the editorial board of the literary review, *Unión.* Since 1959 he has represented the Cuban people on a variety of diplomatic-cultural missions, traveling throughout the republics of eastern Europe and to Viet-Nam, China, and the Soviet Union.

2. Apart from his achievements as a poet, Guillén has always taken time to participate in important conferences and cultural gatherings in various parts of the world. These have included: the Congress of the League of Revolutionary Writers and Artists (LEAR), Mexico, 1937; the Second International Congress of Writers for the Defense of Culture, Valencia-Barcelona, 1938; the Association of Anti-Fascist Intellectuals, Madrid, 1938; the Cultural and Scientific Congress for Peace, New York, 1949; and the Continental Congress of Culture, Santiago de Chile, 1953. In 1937 he became a Communist and five years later in his home town, Camagüey, represented the Party as an unsuccessful candidate for Mayor. In 1953 he was honored in Moscow by the Stalin Prize. A contributor to Cuban journals since very early in his career, Guillén became through the years a first-class critical journalist. A selection of his articles (1938-1961) has been published as: *Prosa de prisa: crónicas* (Santa Clara: Universidad Central de Las Villas, 1962), and reprinted the following year in Buenos Aires by Editorial Hernández.

tions on the politics of his *oeuvre* would be no less germane.

Neither would it be particularly useful to characterize what Guillén has accomplished as *engagé* or militant. While these facile clichés can be applied to his poetry or, now and again, to the work of a few other modern artists, they are equally accurate with respect to the Lord's Prayer and the Monroe Doctrine. Militancy, as history so painfully demonstrates, has never been an exclusive province of those who share Guillén's world-view.

Concerning that world-view, it would be most exact to begin by calling the man a leftist. That is, in both intention and execution, his work is implacably antibourgeois or, what amounts in today's world to the same thing, anticapitalist. Even beyond this—and herein lies perhaps its greatest distinction—the poetry of Nicolás Guillén is revolutionary. But the revolution here is no simple matter of language, style, or form: that distracting swarm of "isms" which identifies the bulk of twentieth-century writing, and which may well emerge in the final analysis as historical curiosity, has not touched Guillén. In contrast to the majority of modern antibourgeois poets, he is direct, accessible, and, in the finest sense of the word, popular. Moreover, he has managed to apprehend and address himself to what one recent essay calls "the collective need for poetry in certain historical periods (the German occupation of France, for example) and in certain social situations (at rallies and demonstrations) when the group wants both to manifest and to structure its unity, its demands and its enthusiasm."[3]

April 20, 1930, marks Guillén's first response to that need, the debut of his revolutionary verse. On that day, *Ideales de una Raza,* the Sunday literary page of an otherwise conservative Havana newspaper, *Diario de la Marina,* published his *Motivos de Son* [*Son Motifs*]. "As soon as these poems had entered the cultural life of our island," writes critic-biographer Angel Augier, "we had the joyful sensation of discovering the essence of our own

3. Michel Beaujour, "Flight out of Time: Poetic Language and the Revolution," *Literature and Revolution,* Jacques Ehrmann, ed. (Boston: Beacon Press, 1967), 30

lyricism. . . . The *son,* a passionate dance born out of the Negro-white encounter under Caribbean skies in which the words and music of the people culiminate in song, is the basic substance of the elemental poetry which Guillén intuitively felt as the expression of the Cuban spirit. . . . He specifically chose the *son* as the mixed artistic creation of the two races that make up the Cuban population for the *son,* in form and content, runs the full gamut of every aspect of our national character."[4]

While it has always been plain to the point of commonplace that Cuba is a lively protean synthesis, so to speak, of the white Spanish thesis and the black African antithesis, no one before Guillén had advanced such a bold affirmation of the latter. Among the few Negroes who had managed in the nineteenth century to achieve some standing in Cuban letters—Juan Francisco Manzano and Gabriel de la Concepción Valdes (Plácido), for example— the tendency was to assimilate the Spanish colonial culture, to "bleach out" any strains of a darker sensibility. The twentieth century, of course, brought a deepening self-consciousness among Blacks and that much-commented white cultivation of things African and Afro-American, both of which flowered—in genuine as well as pretended manifestations—during the post-World-War-One decade in Harlem and Paris. On a popular level, Cuba's association with this flowering is through the Afro-Caribbean movement which sprang up in Hispanic poetry around the mid-twenties. But the inaugurators of the movement (Luís Palés Matos, a Puerto Rican, and the Cubans, José Zacarías Tallet and Ramón Guirao) were white. Their achievement lay principally in the manipulation of exotic-sounding onomatopoeia and so-called primitive rhythm—a figure they commonly depicted is the stereotypical Black of mystery, sensuality, and dance. They were selective observers (even exploiters) of, rather

4. "The Cuban Poetry of Nicolás Guillén," *Phylon,* XII (1951), 32. This is probably the most helpful article in English on the poet and his development up to the late forties. For a more scholarly account of the sources and evolution of the *son,* see: Alejo Carpentier, *La música en Cuba* (México, D.F.: Fondo de Cultura Económica [Colección Tierra Firme-19], 1946); and Fernando Ortíz, *La africanía de la música folklórica de Cuba* (La Habana: Publicaciones del Ministerio de Educación, Dirección de Cultura, 1950).

than participants in, the world their verse purported to
evoke.

In radical contrast to this local-color approach, Guillén's
eight "*son*-poems" offered a provocative inside picture.
It is the black inhabitant of Havana's slums who speaks
here; what is more, he uses the argot and nonstandard
pronunciation peculiar to his milieu, and sketches
phenomena of his own daily existence. The result is a
new and shocking authenticity. But gradually, through re-
peated confrontations with the text, it becomes clear that,
just behind these entertaining and often happy-go-lucky
slices of ghetto life, the people of *Motivos de Son* (1) do
not have enough to eat, (2) are often ashamed of identi-
fiably Negroid features or coloring, and (3) commonly
live in exploitative sexual promiscuity. One poem tells of a
chulo, or small-time pimp, who is compensated for his
nickname, "Nigger-lips," by a good white suit, two-tone
shoes, and the fact that he lives well without ever work-
ing. In another a woman is told to cheer up and try to
pawn her electric iron because the power is shut off for
nonpayment and the cupboard as well as her man's
pockets are empty. And in one more a woman announces
that, since her man steps out in fine clothes and new
shoes while she sits at home eating rice and biscuits, she
will defy the censure of neighbors and leave him for some-
one else.

Social criticism implicit in these poems, then, finds its ob-
ject in the unpleasant reality they evoke, not in the indi-
viduals who are forced to live it. As regards these latter,
Guillén's affection is unmistakable; so is his admiration
for the spirited and inventive manner in which they con-
front second- and third-class citizenship. On questions
of color gradation among nonwhites, the first four lines of
"My Little Woman" reveal the poet's attitude as one of
healthy racial affirmation. Similarly positive is the piece
in which a man responds to the derisory remarks of a
light-brown woman. The individual in question is far from
offended at having his flat nose likened to the knot of a
necktie, and he assures the author of the comparison
that with a fine black woman at home he need have nothing to do with the likes of her. Finally, Guillén also included an entertaining little piece in which a local fellow,

Bito Manué (Victor Manuel), is teased good-naturedly for attempting a flirtation with an apparently-willing American tourist, when the best he can manage in English is counting to three with a horrible accent. Given both the island's national reality and the poet's concern for authenticity within the limitations of *Motivos de Son*, at least this sort of passing reference to the United States is almost inevitable; undeniably, that country has been the greatest single "outside" influence on the unfolding of the above-mentioned Cuban synthesis. Soon enough Guillén will take more careful note of the United States influence and incorporate a progressive critique of it into his poetry. For the time being, however, imperialism is merely linguistic; there is no real exploitation, only embarrassment.

The immature, highly personal, and *modernista*-inspired verse in which Guillén had dabbled without much distinction during the twenties has become clearly now a thing of the past. That single newspaper page of *Diario de la Marina* at once marks his real self-discovery as a poet and anticipates so much of what he will become. Carefully and surely, he moved from the urban black themes of *Motivos de son* to a more general, national concern in *Sóngoro Cosongo* (1931), then beyond to the broader Caribbean vision which shapes *West Indies Ltd.* (1934). In *Cantos para soldados y sones para turistas* (1937) [*Songs for Soldiers and Sones for Tourists*] he is continental in scope; some months later, with *España: poema en cuatro angustias y una esperanza* (1937) [*Spain: A Poem in Four Anguishes and a Hope*], his perspective has become international. After a decade of silence, *El son entero* (1947) [*The Entire Son*] appeared. Here the poet is revealed in his full thematic, formal, and ideological maturity; he is able to speak concretely to Cuba and the rest of Latin America, while conceding nothing with regard to universality. *La paloma de vuelo popular—Elegías* (1958) [*The Dove of Popular Flight—Elegies*], most of which was composed in exile, contains some of Guillén's most vigorous poems of praise and condemnation; in them he is more explicit than ever before as to his concept of complete social justice and the means of realizing it in today's world. And finally, *Tengo* (1964) [*I Have*], *El gran zoo* (1967) [*The Great Zoo*], and the as yet uncollected *La rueda dentada* [*The Serrated Wheel*] comprehend a hearty poetic endorsement of Cuba's new reality, a determined absorption in the day-to-day tasks and long-range goals of the Revolution.[5]

All along this poetic itinerary Guillén has demonstrated an uncommon versatility. Beyond the *son,* his formal mastery extends to the *décima,* the *letrilla,* and the *romance,* as well as the sonnet, the ballad, and free verse. His ability to blend and juxtapose these forms effectively is evinced in the richly suggestive *Elegies.* If in such poems as "Governor," "Little Rock," and "Short Grotesque Litany on the Death of Senator McCarthy" Guillén is caustic or malicious, others like "Bars," "Paul Éluard," and "Sunday Reading" indicate his capacity for human affection. While "The Flowers Grow High" and, indeed, a great portion of the poet's work is intensely public, such pieces as "Exile" and "Little Ballad of Plovdiv" find him more quietly personal. "Sputnik 57" is a reaction to the scientific present; "My Last Name" explores an unrecorded past. If there is mordant condemnation in "Wu-Sang-Kuei" and "Whatever Time is Past was Worse," there is spirited praise in "Five Chinese Songs" and "Thus Sings a Mockingbird in El Turquino." The coldness and severity of "Mau-Maus" or "Execution" is balanced by the vibrance and warm sensuality of "Ovenstone," "Ana María" or "Words in the Tropics." And while "Soviet Union" is specific and partisan, the spirit of "Sell Me?" is more general and nonsectarian. All this is not simply to assure

5. The rough sketch of Guillén's trajectory, through *El son entero,* was suggested by Augier, 33-4. That essay, along with his much more ambitious two-volume study, *Nicolás Guillén: notas para un estudio biográfico-crítico* (Santa Clara: Universidad Central de Las Villas, 1965), were essential to the preparation of this introduction. The most up-to-date, short piece on Guillén in Spanish is: Robert Márquez, "Introducción a Guillén," *Casa de Las Américas,* XI, 65-6 (marzo-junio, 1971), 136-42, which was originally written, in English, as a preface to *Patria o Muerte: The Great Zoo & Other Poems by Nicolás Guillén: 1928-1969* (New York: October House, 1972). The most recent, thorough biographical-critical study in French is: *Nicolás Guillén,* presentation, choix de textes et traduction par Claude Couffon (Paris: Pierre Seghers, 1964). The best recent piece on the earlier poetry is by Alfred Melon, "Guillén: poeta de las síntesis," *Unión,* no. 4, año 9 (December 1970), pp. 96-132.

the reader there is "something for everyone" in the work of Nicolás Guillén, but rather to underscore the richness of its texture. For while he maintains a consistent mass appeal, the poet has managed to avoid confusing simplicity with simple-mindedness, the genuinely popular with what is merely ordinary.

On a level of theme and ideology it is useful to recall the racial affirmation, social criticism, and awareness of the United States which marked *Motivos de son.* These three features will continue to identify Guillén's poetry, and observations on their diverse presence in it are instructive with regard to his maturing world-view. Curiously enough, even prior to the publication of *Motivos de son,* the three appear as features of a single poem, "Small Ode to a Black Cuban Boxer." Collected later in *Sóngoro cosongo,* "they were lines of racial exaltation and disjointed rhythm, in which there was as yet nothing of the musical quality which would characterize subsequent production: 'the Negro reigns while boulevards applaud!/ Let the envy of the whites/ know proud, authentic Black!' As you can see, the poet asked little. Soon he would ask more."[6]

What Guillén asks here—beyond his expression of admiration for the skills and triumphs of a particular boxer—is that black people in general take into account, even take advantage of, the "Negro craze" which had begun to make itself felt on the island. Around the same time he published an interview with Langston Hughes who was traveling in Cuba and another with the black Cuban songwriter, Rosendo Ruíz. In the former he praises Hughes' *Weary Blues* and *Fine Clothes to the Jew,* and commends his self-conscious blackness as the new stimulating ingredient in American verse. In the latter he chides Cubans for their indiscriminate acceptance of whatever happens to reach them from Paris or New York, and counsels a reacquaintance with and new respect for their own and necessarily mulatto, expressions of popular culture.

6. Nicolás Guillén, from a talk given to the Lyceum Lawn and Tennis Club in Havana, 1945. Quoted by Augier, p. 113. The poem was first published on December 29, 1929, in *Ideales de una Raza.* See: "Kid Chocolate," in our "Notes and Glossary."

The poem in question also makes it plain that, whatever else he might be, this man with "fists of dynamite/ and stylish patent leather shoes" is an easily-exploitable commodity; semiliterate even in his own language, he is trained to perform like "a brand new rubber monkey" for those bored and thrill-seeking crowds up there in "the North." Besides athletes and entertainers, the island has always exported sugar; and this better-known Cuban commodity also whets the appetite of what the poet refers to as "Broadway." Insatiable as the fan at ringside, the exploiter "stretches out its snout, its moist enormous tongue,/ to lick and glut upon/ our canefields vital blood!"

But for the present, Guillén's social criticism and awareness of the United States amount to little more than just that. While he is resentful of certain phenomena on general moral grounds and unassailable in his nationalism, he is not yet involved with thoroughgoing analysis and concrete solutions. As a response to the lionization of his boxer and imperialist incursions in his country, the poet's Marxism is still only incipient.

Not for almost thirty years, until the *Elegies,* will there appear anything quite so total as "Small Ode to a Black Cuban Boxer."[7] Apart from these six extraordinary pieces, the poems as they are selected in the volume in hand exhibit in varying proportions the three features designated as central to Guillén's vision. Racial affirmation is at its most vivid in "Sports," "Words in The Tropics," and "Arrival," while in "Ballad of the Two Grandfathers" and "A *son* for Antillian Children" the poet also takes note of the white European ingredient in his particular admixture. In "I Came on a Slaveship" he is prideful of both who he has been and who he is today. Guillén's response to the presence of the United States in his part of the world varies according to the circumstances in question. He speaks with harsh censure in "Song for Puerto Rico," revolutionary confidence in "Far Off," militant resolve in

7. Those familiar with Guillén's work will, of course, recall that "West Indies Ltd." (1934) expanded and added to the themes of "Small Ode to a Black Cuban Boxer," and hinted at the ideology which would emerge forcefully in the *Elegies.*

"The Flowers Grow High," and triumphant celebration in "Thus Sings a Mockingbird in El Turquino." Social criticism, of course, is one of the more persistent elements of the poet's work. Particularly effective in this area are "Carioca Song," "Mau-Maus," and "Little Rock," while the readiness to temper his criticism with hope and encouragement is plain in "Brazil-Copacabana," "Neighborhood House," and "A Black Man Sings in New York City."

The *Elegies,* conceived and perfected over a period of ten years, were published (together with *La paloma de vuelo popular*) in Buenos Aires only weeks before Fulgencio Batista fled Cuba and "the decisive bearded ones from the Sierra" entered the city of Havana. While some audiences are likely to find these poems almost "heavy," too concentrated, and wanting in polemical subtlety, a close reading of them as well as some sensitivity toward their contexts will be essential to a full appreciation of who and what the poet is. "Elegy for Camagüey" is primarily an engaging, nostalgic tribute to the people and events of yesterday, of the poet's youth. But when he calls: "People of daily needs/ . . . limpid, quotidian, unheroic/ souls: bedrock of history:/ know I speak and dream of you," he is identifying specifically with the common people of his home town and, by implication, with common people everywhere.

In "Elegy for Emmett Till" Guillén speaks with rage and indignation to an unpardonable act of savagery. A poignant juxtaposition of the victim's youth and vulnerability . with the hellish brutality of the locale is accompanied by the plain allegation that this "ancient river, brother to the Black" has borne witness to a good many more incidents of the same nature.

Without question "My Last Name" will stand as one of the poet's most quietly moving and sensitively conducted pieces. It is a pilgrimage beyond the "notary's ink" from which "I know there will come distant cousins," an excavation of "my subterranean galleries/ with great moist rocks/ . . . where I feel the pure rush/ of ancient waters." Reaching into his deepest self and, at the same time, far beyond himself to the multitudes who have the same or an analogous racial composition, Guillén's discovery is: "My name, foreign,/ free and mine, foreign and yours,/ foreign and free as the air." The poem's subtitle could not be more apt; this is, in the broadest sense of the word, a "family elegy."

What was hinted at or barely initiated in "Small Ode to a Black Cuban Boxer" is brought surely to fruition with the elegies dedicated to Cuba, Jacques Roumain, and Jesús Menéndez. The first of these introduces the poet's country as a "sold-out palm grove,/ drawn and quartered dream,/ tough map of sugar and neglect," and attributes the barely tolerable conditions of existence there to "the bloodthirsty eagle/ that from the terrible North brings/ death—maggots and death, a cross and death,/ . . . predictable a priori death,/ rehearsed in Las Vegas/ with a deluge of planes and bombs."

The second recalls trivial as well as serious data of a man, "Monsieur Jacques Roumain,/ who spoke for the black/ Emperor, the black King,/ the black President,/ . . . Blacks not even born:/ . . . anxious, tearing, primary,/ swampy, vegetable flesh." At the same time it evokes pages from Haiti's blood-stained history and champions Roumain's dream of that country's liberation.

The third, like "Elegy for Emmett Till," is occasioned by a crime. Here, a well-liked and highly successful organizer of sugar cane workers was murdered by a Cuban army officer early in 1948. To mark this almost commonplace historical fact, the poet has erected "a grand, mysterious and vegetal mural, a fresco of dark rough colors, human and sacrificial, full of cane fields and gangsters, blood and hope."[8] In doing so, he deftly exploits the specificity of the event as well as its ability to suggest continental and, by extension, third-world reality. That is, the Jesús Menéndez of his poem is at once that black Cuban who was shot at Manzanillo and a force, a sort of "wind that rises from the depths of the ocean, whips through the cane fields, resounds like a shout at daybreak, howls like a panther inside the New York Stock Exchange, ex-

8. Ezequel Martínez-Estrada, *La poesía afrocubana de Nicolás Guillén* (Montevideo: Editorial ARCA, 1966), p. 92.

plodes like a thunderclap, and glows at last with sulphurous morning light."[9]

By this time the full ideological thrust of the poet's writing is plain. Against what he has come to understand as United States capitalism and its colonialist oppression, particularly of Cuba and the other Latin American republics, he calls for revolution. Such names as Martí, Maceo, Dessalines, Peralejo, La Citadelle—people and places from earlier chapters of the same struggle for liberation—are evoked by way of inspiration; and such others as Rochambeau, LeClerc, Walker, and Trujillo are uttered with contempt. Clearly, Guillén is advocating just the sort of revolution which will triumph in Cuba almost immediately upon the publication of these *Elegies*, a revolution fought and won for those "slow, submerged, viscous peoples who die/ like animals, in hospitals and delirium,/ dreaming of life," one to transform "a torn and blinded countryside, vomiting/ its shadows on the road beneath the lash/ of a field boss."

The relationship of the poems collected here to what was termed earlier the group's need "to manifest and to structure its unity, its demands and its enthusiasm" is mainly one of guidance, encouragement. Through them a unity is more clearly perceived, demands further concretized, and enthusiasm proclaimed. In this way they can be seen as members of that large family which includes national anthems, hymns, prayers, pledges, union songs, and even some religious or political oratory. While this sort of expression has its deepest roots in what is understood as poetry, it is most often indifferent to traditional academic standards of poetic excellence. That is, one's response to the anthem or the prayer, as well as to these poems, will be largely contingent on his particular relationship to the phenomena they evoke. Aesthetic considerations—though here joined inextricably and effectively to the extra-literary end—will come later. In any case, even among those not that closely connected to the phenomena evoked by the poems, the response is not likely to be completely neutral. For, operating as they do in the sphere of everyday civic reality, they cannot help but touch many more,

9. Ibid., p. 90-1.

far beyond the immediate recipients of their guidance and encouragement. If that touch wounds, draws blood, then Nicolás Guillén has been doubly successful.

Man-making Words

Exilio

El Sena
discurre circunspecto;
civilizada linfa
que saluda en silencio,
sacándose el sombrero.
Mi patria en el recuerdo
y yo en París clavado
como un blando murciélago.
¡Quiero
el avión que me lleve,
con sus cuatro motores
y un solo vuelo!

Brilla sangre en el pecho
de esa nube que pasa
lenta, en el bajo cielo.
Va de negro. La hieren
cuatro cuchillos nuevos.
Viene del Mar Caribe,
pirata mar caníbal,
duro mar de ojos ciegos
y asesinado sueño.
¡Volver con esa nube
y sus cuatro cuchillos
y su vestido negro!

Ríos

Tengo del Rin, del Ródano, del Ebro,
tengo los ojos llenos;
tengo del Tíber y del Támesis,
tengo del Volga, del Danubio,
tengo los ojos llenos.

Pero yo sé que el Plata,
pero yo sé que el Amazonas baña;
pero yo sé que el Misisipi,
pero yo sé que el Magdalena baña;
yo sé que el Almendares,
pero yo sé que el San Lorenzo baña;
yo sé que el Orinoco,
pero yo sé que bañan
tierras de amargo limo donde mi voz florece

Exile

The Seine,
cultured lymph,
flows circumspect
and nods quietly,
removing its hat.
My country in my memory
and I in Paris on display
like a harmless bat.
Oh, for the plane
to take me
with four motors
on a single flight!

Blood shines on the breast
of a cloud that moves
slow in the overcast sky.
Dressed in mourning,
rent by four recent knives,
it's from the *Mar Caribe*
. . . a pirate, cannibal sea,
a tough sea of sightless eyes
and murdered sleep.
Oh, to return with that cloud,
her four knives,
and dress of mourning!

Rivers

With the Rhine, the Rhone, the Ebro,
my eyes are filled.
With the Tiber, the Thames,
the Volga, the Danube,
my eyes are filled.

But I know the Plata,
and I know the Amazon bathes.
But I know the Mississippi,
and I know the Magdalena bathes.
I know the Almendares,
and I know the San Lorenzo bathes.
I know the Orinoco,
I know they bathe
lands of bitter slime where my voice blooms,

3

y lentos bosques presos en sangrientas raíces.
¡Bebo en tu copa, América,
en tu copa de estaño,
anchos ríos de lágrimas!

Dejad, dejadme,
dejadme ahora junto al agua.

Bares

Amo los bares y tabernas
junto al mar,
donde la gente charla y bebe
sólo por beber y charlar.
Donde Juan Nadie llega y pide
su trago elemental,
y están Juan Bronco y Juan Navaja
y Juan Narices y hasta Juan
Simple, el sólo, el simplemente
Juan.

Allí la blanca ola
bate de la amistad;
una amistad de pueblo, sin retórica,
una ola de ¡hola! y ¿cómo estás?
Allá huele a pescado,
a mangle, a ron, a sal
y a camisa sudada puesta a secar al sol.

Búscame, hermano, y me hallarás
(en La Habana, en Oporto,
en Jacmel, en Shanghai)
con la sencilla gente
que sólo por beber y charlar
puebla los bares y tabernas
junto al mar.

and languid jungles chained by bloody roots.
America, I drink from your cup,
from your tin cup,
great rivers of tears!

Oh, leave me, leave me,
leave me now
. . . close to the water.

Bars

How I love the bars and taverns
near the sea
where people drink and talk
just to talk and drink.
Where John Nobody comes and calls
for an ordinary drink,
and in come John Harshvoice, John Straightrazor,
John Spadenose, and even John Simple
. . . plain and simple
John.

That's where a white wave foams with friendship;
a peoples' friendship, one without rhetoric:
a wave of "Hey," of "What's happening?"
That's where it smells of fish,
mangrove, rum, salt,
and a sweaty shirt out drying in the sun.

So come by, brother, and you'll find me
(in La Habana, Oporto,
Jacmel, Shanghai)
with ordinary people
who just to drink and talk
people the bars and taverns
near the sea.

Ciudades

Kingston

Bajo el hambriento sol
(God save the King)
negra de bata blanca
cantando una canción.
(God save the King)
Una canción.
¿Por siempre?
¿Por siempre esa canción?
Oh yes!
Oh no!
Oh yes!

Oh no!

New York

¿Y la tarde, entreabierta
como una niña pura?
¿Y el corazón, decidme?
¿Habéis visto una lágrima?

Panamá

—How are you, Panamá?
—I'm well,
(El cabaret de Jimmy, el bar de Joe.)
—¿Sí?
—Yes.

Hermano panameño:
¿No sueñas con Hostos y Martí?
—Sueño.
—Yes?
—Sí.

Cities

Kingston

Beneath the starving sun
(God save the King)
a black girl dressed in white,
singing a song
(God save the King).
A song.
Forever?
That song forever?
Oh yes!
Oh no!
Oh yes!

Oh no!

New York

And late afternoon, open
as a young girl?
And her heart . . . tell me,
have you seen the tears?

Panama

How are you, Panama?
Very well.
(Joe's Bar and Jimmy's Cabaret).
Yes?
Sí.

Brother Panamanian,
don't you dream of Hostos and Martí?
I dream.
Yes?
Sí!

Madrid

Bajo el azufre polvoriento,
un miliciano muerto,
un joven muerto, ya viejo,
se saca un árbol del pecho.
—¿Has entendido?
            —Entiendo.

São Paulo

Saltas de puente en puente
y sueñas con un río,
como una solterona
que espera en vano a un hijo.
Tú, llena de puentes secos
sobre el gentío.

Canción carioca

¿Te hablaron ya de Río,
del Pan, del Corcovado
y el sanguinario estío?
            ¿Te han hablado?

De la *boite* encendida
y el salón apagado,
del verdor de la vida,
            ¿te han hablado?

Del Carnaval rupestre,
semental desbocado,
rojo arcángel terrestre,
            ¿te han hablado?

Del mar y la campaña,
del cielo repujado,
que ni una nube empaña,
            ¿te han hablado?

Yo te hablo de otro Río:
del Río de Janeiro

Madrid

Beneath sulphuric clouds
a dead militia-man,
a youth already old lies dead.
A tree grows from his breast.
Do you understand?
I understand.

São Paulo

You leap from bridge to bridge
and dream of rivers,
like a spinster
hopes in vain to have a son.
You, so full of sterile spans
above the crowd.

Carioca Song

Have you heard yet of Rio,
of Sugarloaf, of Corcovado
and the sanguinary summer?
            Have you heard?

Of the flaming *boite*
and the dim salon,
of life's abundance,
            have you heard?

Of the rupestrian Carnival,
a stallion runaway,
terrestial red archangel,
            have you heard?

Of the sea, the countryside,
the polished sky,
not a cloud to stain it,
            have you heard?

I speak of another Rio:
of Rio de Janeiro:

de no-techo, sí-frío,
hambre-sí, no-cruzeiro.

Del llanto sin pañuelo,
del pecho sin escudo,
de la trampa y el vuelo,
de la soga y el nudo.

El *jazz* en el *soirée*
sacude el aire denso;
yo pienso en el café
(y lloro cuando pienso.)

Mas pienso en la *favela*.
La vida allí estancada
es un ojo que vela.
Y pienso en la alborada.

¿Te hablaron ya de Río,
con su puñal clavado
en el pecho sombrío?
                    ¿Te han hablado?

Brazil—Copacabana   Copacabana.
Bajo el sol brasileño,
es como un blanco sueño
la mañana.
          Ingleses.
          Argentinos.
          Franceses.
          Tunecinos.
          Yanquis (siempre vecinos
          del bar . . .)
¿Y esa hembra dorada,
que está en la arena echada,
espera acaso un golpe masculino del mar?

no-roof, cold-yes,
hunger-yes, no-cruzeiro.

Of never-drying tears,
chests without a shield,
of traps and flight,
of noose and neck.

The *soiree's* jazz
stirs the heavy air;
I think of coffee
(and when I think I weep).

I think of the *favela*.
The life imprisoned there
is but a watchful eye.
And I think of the dawn.

Have you heard yet of Rio,
its dagger nailed
to its somber chest?
                Have you heard?

Brazil—Copacabana   Copacabana.
The morning
a crystal dream
beneath the Brazilian sun.
        Englishmen.
        Argentines.
        Frenchmen.
        Tunisians.
        Yankees (always
        by the bar . . .)
Could that tanned woman,
lying on the sand,
be waiting for the masculine surge of the sea?

Telón

Noche. Samba. Dancings. Whiskey. Mar Negro.
Mujeres que se deslizan
como sombras en un espejo.
Esto es
una coctelera endiablada,
en la que un *barman* de pesadilla
bate hierro y cemento,
agua de mar con hiel.
Y sangre, que hace el papel
de alcohol en este cóctel.
¡Oh el concéntrico encanto
de no pensar en el llanto!
(¡Allá los que no piensen en él!)

Oigo casas, se oyen las casas
en un estruendo de metal
disparado hacia el firmamento.
¡Son casas en pecado mortal!
¿Y en los morros, qué tal?
Hombre,
pues en los morros,
como siempre,
muy mal.

Mientras de piso en piso
sube, se repite la piedra
y adustos bronces condecoran
las ambiciosas galerías,
poseídas
como sonrosadas queridas,
yo sueño
bajo el sol brasileño.

¿Dónde lo vi?
¡Dios mío, si es un sueño que vi
en Moscú
y en Bulgaria
y en Bratislava
y en Praga
y en Rumania
y en Polonia
y en Budapest!

Curtain

Night. Samba. Dancing halls. Whiskey. Black Sea.
Women that slip away
like shadows in a mirror.
This is
a hellish cocktail shaker,
in which a nightmare barman
mixes cement and iron,
sea water with bile.
And blood, this cocktail's alcohol.
Oh, the concentric enchantment
of not thinking on the tears!
(Let those who forget them beware!)

I hear houses, houses heard
in a clatter of metal
shot towards the firmament.
Houses in mortal sin!
And the slums on the hill?
Well, sir,
in the slums,
as usual,
very bad.

While it rises floor by floor,
the stone resounds
and harsh tans decorate
ambitious galleries,
possessed
like blushing mistresses,
I dream
beneath the Brazilian sun.

Where'd I see it?
My god, why it's a dream I saw
in Moscow
and Bulgaria
and Bratislava
and Prague,
in Rumania
and Poland
and Budapest!

Lo vi en la Habana.
Lo vi, no lo soñé.
Palacios de antiguo mármol
para el que vivió sin zapatos.
Castillos donde el obrero reposa
sentado a la diestra de su obra.
El cigarral de la duquesa
para la hija de Juan, que está enferma.
La montaña y la playa y el vichy y el caviar
para los que antes no tenían donde estar.

¿Y aquí en Copacabana, aquí?
También lo vi.
Pues aunque todavía
es un sueño,
siento venir el día
ha de llegar el día,
se oye rugir el día
con el viento nordeste de Pernambuco y de Bahía,
un día de sangre y pólvora bajo el sol brasileño.

**La pequeña balada
de Plóvdiv**

Bulgaria

En la vieja villa de Plóvdiv,
        lejos, allá,
mi corazón murió una noche
        y nada más.

Una larga mirada verde,
        lejos, allá,
húmedos labios prohibidos
        y nada más.

El cielo búlgaro brillaba,
        lejos, allá,
lleno de estrellas temblorosas
        y nada más.

¡Oh, lentos pasos en la calle,
        lejos, allá,
últimos pasos para siempre
        y nada más!

I saw it in Havana.
I saw it, it was no dream.
Palaces of ancient marble
for those who had no shoes.
Castles where the worker rests
sitting on the right of his own labor.
The country house of the Duchess
for John's daughter, who is sick.
The mountain, the beach, the vichy, the caviar
for those who had no place before.

And here, here in Copacabana?
I saw it too.
For even though
it's still a dream,
I feel the day is coming,
the day will come,
you can hear it roar
with the northeast wind from Pernambuco and Bahía,
a day of blood and gunpowder beneath the Brazilian sun.

**The Little Ballad
of Plovdiv**

Bulgaria

In the ancient town of Plovdiv,
    far off, before,
my heart died late one night
    and nothing more.

A lingering, verdant gaze,
    far off, before,
her moist, forbidden lips
    and nothing more.

Bulgarian skies above,
    far off, before,
lit by trembling stars
    and nothing more.

Gentle steps along the street,
    far off, before,
final footsteps, never again
    and nothing more.

Junto a la puerta misteriosa,
lejos, allá,
la mano blanca, un solo beso
y nada más.

En el invierno de París

Palabras para un
couplet dedicado al
abate Pierre, que
protegía a los
indigentes del frío

En el invierno de París
la pasan mal
los sans-abris;
la pasan mal
los sans-logis;
la pasan mal
los sans-nourri:
la pasan mal
en el invierno de París.

En el invierno de París
¿qué piensas tu,
sin un ami?
¿Qué piensas tú
Solo en la rue?
¿Qué piensas tú
de mí, de tí,
qué piensas tú,
en el invierno de París?

En el invierno de París
viene el burgués
(que ama la vie)
viene el burgués
y exclama: oui!
Viene el burgués,
repite: oui!
Viene el burgués
en el invierno de París.

En el invierno de París
nunca se vio
gente tan chic;
nunca se vio
tan fino esprit;
nunca se vio

Close by the mysterious gate,
                    far off, before,
her hand so white, a single kiss
                    and nothing more.

In the Winter in Paris

Words for a couplet
dedicated to the abbot
Pierre, who protected
the indigent from the
cold

In the winter in *Paris*
the *sans-abris*
fair badly;
the *sans-logis*
fair badly;
the *sans-nourri*
fair badly
in the winter in *Paris.*

In the winter in *Paris*
what do you think,
with no *ami?*
What do you think
Seul on the *rue?*
What do you think
of me, of you,
what do you think
in the winter in *Paris?*

In the winter in *Paris*
the bourgeois comes
(who loves *la vie*)
the bourgeois comes,
and exclaims: *oui!*
The bourgeois comes,
and repeats: *oui!*
The bourgeois comes
in the winter in *Paris.*

In the winter in *Paris*
you never saw
people so *chic;*
you never saw
such fine *esprit;*
you never saw

la bas o ici,
nunca se vio
en el invierno de París.

En el invierno de París
con calma pues
tendrás abris;
con calma pues
serás nourri;
con calma pues
se dice (on dit)
con calma pues
en el invierno de París.

En el invierno de París
vivir podrás
un mes así;
vivir podrás
con lait, con lit;
vivir podrás
ya sans souci;
vivir podrás
en el invierno de París.

En el invierno de París . . .
¿Pero y después?
Solo en la rue.
¿Pero y después?
Sin un ami.
¿Pero y después?
Ni lait ni lit.
¿Pero y después
sin el invierno de París?

Casa de vecindad

Sola, sobre su ola de parado coral,
Antillilandia vive,
esperando el trompetazo del Juicio Inicial.

Casa de Vecindad, patio del Mar Caribe,
donde los inquilinos se juntan
bajo la luna, para charlar de sus cosas;

la bas or *ici,*
you never saw
in the winter in *Paris.*

In the winter in *Paris*
have patience then
you'll have *abris;*
have patience then
you'll be *nourri;*
have patience then
they say *(on dit)*
have patience then
in the winter in *Paris.*

In the winter in *Paris*
you'll live that way
one week plus three;
you'll live that way
with *lait,* with *lit;*
you'll live that way
now *sans-souci;*
you'll live that way
in the winter in *Paris.*

In the winter in *Paris . . .*
What after that?
Seul on the *rue.*
What after that?
With no *ami.*
What after that?
No *lait,* no *lit.*
What after that
with no winter in *Paris?*

Neighborhood House

Alone, on her wave of standing coral,
lives Antilleland,
waiting for the trumpet blast of The First Judgment.

Neighborhood house, patio to the Caribbean,
where tenants gather beneath the moon to chat;
where now there are Negroes to question

donde hay ya negros que preguntar
y mujeres que asesinaron sus mariposas.
Onda negribermeja
de obreros de agria ceja
y niños con la cara vieja,
heridos por el ojo fijo del policía.
Tierra donde la sangre ensucia el día
y hay pies en detenida velocidad de salto
y gargantas de queja y no de grito
y gargantas de grito y no de queja
y voces de cañaverales en alto
y lo que se dice y no está escrito
y todo lo demás que ya sabremos
a medida que andemos.

Casa de vecindad, patio del Mar Caribe,
con mi guitarra de áspero son,
aquí estoy, para ver si me saco del pecho
una canción.
Una canción de sueño desatado,
una simple canción de muerte y vida
con que saludar el futuro ensangrentado,
rojo como las sábanas, como los muslos, como el lecho
de una mujer recién parida.

Unión Soviética

Jamás he visto un *trust* soviético en mi patria.
Ni un banco.
Ni tampoco un *ten cents.*
Ni un central.
Ni una estación naval.
Ni un tren.
Nunca jamás hallé
un campo de bananas
donde al pasar leyera:
MÁSLOV AND COMPANY, S. EN C.
PLÁTANOS AL POR MAYOR. OFICINAS EN CUBA:
MACEO ESQUINA CON NO-SÉ-QUÉ.
Ni un cable así:
Moscú, noviembre 15 (UPI).
Ayer los crudos se mantuvieron firmes.

and women who've murdered their butterflies.
Blackish-red wave of workers with bitter brows
and children with old faces,
wounded by the policeman's piercing eye.
Land where blood defiles the day
and legs are frozen in their leaping speed,
with throats complaining and not screaming
and throats screaming and not in complaint
and canefield voices raised
and what's said and isn't written
and all the rest we'll know
as we move on.

Neighborhood house, patio to the Caribbean,
Here I am with my harsh-*son* guitar,
trying to bring out a song.
A song of frenzied dreaming,
a simple song of death and life
with which to greet the future drenched in blood,
red as the sheets, as the thighs,
as the bed
of a woman who's just given birth.

Soviet Union

Never have I seen a Soviet trust in my country.
Nor a bank,
a ten cents,
a central,
a naval base,
or a train.
I've never once found
a banana plantation
where on passing you might read:
MÁSLOV AND COMPANY, INC.
WHOLESALE BANANAS. OFFICES IN CUBA:
CORNER OF MACEO AND SUCH-AND-SUCH A STREET.
Never a cable like this:
Moscow, November 15 (UPI).
Yesterday common stock remained steady.

Ni de allá
la insinuación más fina, más ligera
de inmiscuir aquella nieve tan conocida
en nuestra conocida primavera.

Viajé en ferrocarril.
(Vuelvo a hablar de la URSS.)
Y nunca vi
Para blancos.—Para negros.
Ni en el bus,
ni en el café.
Para blancos.—Para negros.
Ni en el bar,
ni en el restaurant.
Para blancos.—Para negros.
Ni en el hotel,
ni en el avión.
Para blancos.—Para negros.
Ni en el amor,
ni en el plantel.
Para blancos.—Para negros.
Ni de allá gente que aquí llegara
y la mano cordial no nos tendiera
sin preguntar si era la piel oscura o clara.

En nuestro mar nunca encontré
piratas de Moscú.
(Hable, Caribe, usted.)
Ni de Moscú tampoco, en mis claras bahías
ese ojo-radar super atento
las noches y los días
queriendo adivinar mi pensamiento.
Ni bloqueo
Ni *marines.*
Ni lanchas para infiltrar espías.
¿Barcos soviéticos? Muy bien.
Son petroleros, mire usted.
Son pescadores, sí, señor
Otros llevan azúcar, traen café
junto a fragantes ramos de esperanzas en flor.
Yo, poeta, lo digo:
Nunca de allá nos vino nada
sin que tuviera el suave gusto del pan amigo,
el sabor generoso de la voz camarada.

And never from there
the slightest, whispering threat
of meddling in the well-known snow
of our familiar spring.

I went by train
(speaking again of the USSR)
and never saw
White Only—Colored Only.
Nor on the bus
or in a cafe,
White Only—Colored Only.
Nor in a bar
or at a restaurant,
White Only—Colored Only.
Nor in a hotel
or on a plane,
White Only—Colored Only.
Nor in love
or at school,
White Only—Colored Only.
Nor from there has come a soul
who neglects to extend a cordial hand
if the skin of the other's not white
but tan.

In our sea I've never found
pirates from Moscow.
(You speak, Caribe!)
Nor from Moscow in my clear bays
that radar-disk, super-attentive
day and night,
its eye fixed on my thoughts.
No blockade either,
or Marines,
or launches to smuggle in spies.
Soviet ships? Very well;
they're tankers, you see.
That's right, and fishing boats.
Others carry sugar, and ship coffee
perfumed by fragrant clusters of blossoming hope.
I, a poet, declare
that never have they sent a thing
without the gentle taste of friendly bread
and generous flavor of a brother's voice.

Union Soviética, cuando del Norte funeral
un áspero viento descendió;
cuando el verdugo dio
una vuelta más al dogal;
cuando empezó su trabajo el gran torturador impasible
y nos quemó las plantas de los pies
para que dijéramos: "Washington, está bien,
elévanos hasta ti";
para que dijéramos lo que no íbamos a decir,
salió tu voz sostenedora, tu gran voz,
de la fábrica y del koljós
y de la escuela y del taller,
y gritó con la nuestra: ¡No!
Juntos así marchamos libres los dos,
frente a un mismo enemigo que habremos de vencer los
     dos.
Toma, pues, Unión Soviética, te lo dejo, toma mi oscuro
corazón de par en par abierto;
ya sabemos por ti cual es el camino seguro,
después de tanto mar ya sabemos por ti dónde está el
     puerto.

El cosmonauta

El cosmonauta, sin saberlo,
arruina el negocio del mito
de Dios sentado atento y fijo
en un butacón inmenso.

¿Qué se han hecho los Tronos y Potencias?
¿Dónde están los Castigos y Obediencias?
¿Y san Crescencio y san Bitongo?
¿Y san Cirilo Zangandongo?
¿Y el fumazo del incienso?
¿Y la fulígine de la mirra?
¿Y las estrellitas pegadas
al cristal ahumado nocturno?
¿Y los arcángeles y los ángeles,
y los serafines y los querubines,
y las Dominaciones en sus escuadrones,
y las vírgenes,
y todos los demás animales afines?

Soviet Union, when bitter winds blew down
from a funereal North,
the executioner gave
the screw a final turn,
and the great implacable torturer started in
to burn the soles of our feet
that we might say, "All right, Washington,
raise us to your level";
that we might say what we would never say—
there rose your hearty voice, your grand voice
from the factory, farm,
school, and shop.
With ours it shouted, "No!"
Thus we march together and free
against an enemy we two will defeat.
Receive, Soviet Union, this dark
and candid heart I offer freely.
Because of you we know the surest course,
and after so much sea where lies the port.

The Cosmonaut

The cosmonaut, unwittingly,
ruins the business of the myth
of God seated, fixed and attentively,
in an immense armchair.

What has become of the Thrones and Powers?
Where are the Punishments and Obediences?
And Saint Crescencio and Saint Bitongo?
And Saint Cirilo Zangandongo?
And the gusts of smoke from the frankincense?
And the fuliginous myrrh?
And the little stars pasted
to the nocturnal stained glass?
And the archangels and angels,
and the seraphs and cherubs,
and the squadrons of angelic beings,
and the virgins,
and other related animals?

El cosmonauta
sigue su pauta.

Sube sube sube
sube sube sube
sube sube sube
sube sube sube
sube.

Deja atrás la última nube.
Rompe el último velo.
El Cielo. El Cielo?
Frío.
El vasto cielo frío.
Hay en efecto un butacón,
pero está vacío.

Sputnik 57

Alta noche en el cielo . . . Sosegado,
como quien vive (y con razón) contento,
sin futuro, presente ni pasado
y en blanco el pensamiento,
duerme Dios en su nube,
situada en lo mejor del Firmamento:
lecho desmesurado,
cama imperial y al mismo tiempo trono,
hecha de lapislázuli dorado,
con adornos de nácar, humo y viento.
Huele a jazmín eléctrico y a ozono.
Del abismo terrestre
el eco amortiguado
confuso y vago sube,
pues filtra, cataloga, desmenuza
todo ruido indiscreto
un gran querube armado,
aunque por regla celestial no es lícito
(y aun se tiene por falta de respeto)
que ande armado un querube.
Ni suaves oraciones,
como puros, blanquísimos pichones
del Espíritu Santo,
ni dobles de campana,

The cosmonaut
follows his route.

Rising rising rising
rising rising rising
rising rising rising
rising rising rising
rising.

Leaving behind the last cloud.
Breaking through the last veil.
The sky. The sky?
It's cold.
The vast cold sky.
There is, in truth, an armchair,
but it's empty.

Sputnik 57

The sky's in total night . . . At peace,
as one who lives (and with some reason) content,
without a future, a present or a past
and with his mind a complete blank,
God sleeps on his cloud,
on the best site in the Firmament:
an immense bed that is also a throne,
made of gilded lapis-lazuli,
with mother-of-pearl, smoke and wind adornments.
There's a scent of electric jasmin and ozone.
From the terrestial void an echo
rises, vague, confused and muffled,
for every sound that's indiscrete
is filtered, catalogued, purified
by a great armed cherub,
though by celestial rule it is illegal
(and is even considered a sign of disrespect)
for a cherub to go armed.
Not gentle prayers,
like pure, like whitest doves
of the Holy Ghost
nor bell tolls that fly sweetly
from the smallest local parish,
dissolving on the city breeze,

de esos que vuelan dulces
de la parroquia mínima,
disueltos en la brisa ciudadana,
o los más poderosos
de las iglesias ricas, las de piedra,
góticas medievales catedrales,
con obispos ociosos,
con obispos golosos y orquestales.
Ni misas, ni sonrisas,
ni ruegos, procesiones y rosarios,
ni siquiera una nota
del órgano profundo,
ni una expresión devota
del millón que escuchamos cada día
brotar del seco corazón del mundo:
nada se arrastra o aleteando sube
hasta el trono de Dios, quien sosegado,
duerme en su enorme nube,
mientras le cuida el sueño un gran querube,
un gran querube armado.

Veloces, los cometas matemáticos
pasan rubios, en ondas sucesivas;
las estrellas monóculas
brillan suspensas en el techo ingrávido;
piafan, caracolean
finos planetas de color oscuro
y en el éter patean
y polvo elevan con el casco puro.
¡Qué fastidio inmortal! Eternamente
Venus en su sayal de lumbre baja,
Aldebarán con su camisa roja,
la Luna a veces queso, otras navaja;
los niños asteroides
y sus viejas nodrizas;
el Sol redondo y bonachón, cenizas
de otros mundos, etcétera.

Es decir, todo el denso
paravant estelar, el toldo inmenso
tras el cual duerme Dios en una nube,
apacible y confiado,
mientras le cuida el sueño un gran querube,
un gran querube armado.

or the more powerful ones
from rich churches, the stone ones,
gothic medieval cathedrals,
with idle bishops,
with gluttonous and orchestral bishops;
not masses nor smiles,
not pleas, processions or rosaries,
not even one note
from the deep organ,
not one devout utterance
of the million we hear every day
come from the world's withered heart:
nothing creeps in or, fluttering, flys up
to the throne of God, who sleeps
peacefully on his enormous cloud,
while a great cherub guards his sleep,
a great armed cherub.

The mathematical comets, glowing,
pass swiftly in successive waves;
the monocular stars glitter
suspended from the weightless ceiling;
they paw and caracole
elegant planets of darkly color
and kick at the sky
and raise dust with their unblemished hooves.
What an immortal nuisance! Venus
eternally in her tunic of muted fire,
Aldebaran in his crimson shirt,
the moon cheese and a knife by turns;
the asteroid children
and their old wet-nurses;
the Sun, round and jolly, the ashes
of other worlds, et cetera.

That is to say, the whole dense stellar
paravent, the immense pomp
behind which God sleeps on a cloud,
peacefully and self-assured,
while a great cherub guards his sleep,
a great armed cherub.

Hasta que Dios despierta . . . Con mirada
seca, de un golpe rápido recorre
su vasto imperio. Cuenta las estrellas,
revisa los planetas y asustada
la voz, pregunta al vigilante angélico:
—¿No habéis notado nada?

He sentido un pequeño
sacudimiento celestial, un leve
chasquido en medio de la augusta niebla
de mi profundo sueño.

—¡Oh, Dios, oh, Padre, oh, Justo! ¡Pura Causa
de la Vida Inmortal! —gimió el querube—,
he visto de aquel astro
(y aquí el querube señaló en la Tierra
el país de granito y esperanza
donde el Kremlin sus álgidos rubíes
sostiene en graves torres),
he visto de aquel astro
una estrella partir. Su rastro breve
era sonoro y fino. Todavía
viaja, está allí. Con encendidas puntas
deja en la noche una impecable estría.
Volvió la vista Dios hacia la zona
donde el globo mecánico
se mueve en que vivimos,
con su nívea corona,
con sus gordos racimos,
el aire (un poco) de sensual matrona.

La Luna, en un sudario de sonetos,
convencional y pálida moría
como siempre. Y huyendo de la Luna,
recién nacida eufórica,
otra luna veloz correr se vía.

Dios contempló indeciso
aquel punto brillante,
aquel astro insumiso,
que se metió en el Cielo sin permiso
y cabizbajo se quedó un instante.
(Un instante de Dios, como se sabe,
es un milenio para el hombre, atado

Until God awakes . . . With a wrinkled face
he surveys his vast empire in one rapid glance.
He counts the stars,
examines the planets and, with startled voice,
inquires of the angelic sentinel:
"Didn't you notice anything?
I felt a small celestial tremor, a slight
crackle in the middle of the august mist
of my deep sleep."

"Oh, God, oh, Father, oh, Just! Pure Cause
of Immortal Life!," the cherub whimpered.
"I saw from that star
(and here the cherub pointed to the Earth,
to the land of hope and granite
where on grave towers the Kremlin
supports its icy rubies)
from that star I saw
a star depart. Its brief trail
was thin and sonorous. There, it is
still traveling. With fiery points
it leaves an impeccable line upon the night.
God turned his face to the zone
where the mechanical globe
in which we live revolves,
with its snowy crown,
with its thick vines,
with the air (a bit) of a sensual matron.

The Moon, with its handkerchief of sonnets,
pale and conventional, was, as usual,
dying. And fleeing from the Moon,
euphoric, newly born,
another moon was swiftly running.

God looked with indecision
at the bright spot,
that insubmissive star,
that came into the sky without permission
and lowered his head for an instant.
(An instant of God, as we know,
is a millenium for man, who is tied

31

a los minutos mínimos, al tiempo
que gotea en la clepsidra . . .) De modo
que Dios aún permanece
silencioso, sentado
en su imponente nube,
donde vela impasible un gran querube,
un gran querube armado.

TELEGRAMAS DE SPELLMAN, EXPEDIDOS
DESDE NEW YORK, ANUNCIAN
ROGATIVAS. VALORES SOSTENIDOS
SE DERRUMBAN. PÁNICO Y EDICIONES
EXTRAS DE LOS PERIÓDICOS. CONSULTAS
AL PENTÁGONO. RADIO—
TELEVISIÓN OFRECE,
EN VEZ DE ASESINATOS Y CANCIONES,
EL DISCURSO DE UN SABIO MELANCÓLICO
QUE PROMETE LA LUNA A FIN DE AÑO
Y LOS VIAJES A HÉRCULES
DENTRO DE DOS, Y UN BAÑO
DE SOL, NO YA EN LA PLAYA
SINO EN EL SOL . . .

Un vasto griterío
(griterío en inglés) estalla y sube
como una nube inmensa hasta la nube
donde está Dios sentado,
con un querube al lado, un gran querube,
un gran querube armado.

¡Oh, Mapamundi, gracia de la escuela!
Cuando en el aula pura
de mi niñez veía
girando tu redonda geografía
pintada de limón y de canela,
reo en una prisión alta y oscura
irremediablemente me sentía.

¿Cómo rasgar un día
de aquella jaula hermética
el sello azul y al cielo interminable
salir donde los astros son ya música
y el cuerpo sombra vagarosa y leve?

to the smallest minutes, to the time
that drops through the hour-glass . . .) Thus
God is still in silence, seated
on his imposing cloud,
where a great cherub is impassively on watch,
a great armed cherub.

TELEGRAMS BY SPELLMAN, SENT OUT
OF NEW YORK, ANNOUNCE PRAYERS.
BLUECHIP STOCKS ARE FALLING.
PANIC AND "EXTRAS" FROM THE NEWSPAPERS.
CONSULTATIONS WITH THE PENTAGON.
RADIO AND TELEVISION OFFER,
INSTEAD OF SONGS AND MURDERS,
THE SPEECH OF A MELANCHOLY SCHOLAR
WHO PROMISES THE MOON BY THE YEAR'S END
AND TRIPS TO HERCULES
WITHIN TWO YEARS, AND A SUN BATH,
NOT ON THE BEACH,
BUT ON THE SUN . . .

A vast outcry
(an outcry in English) bursts and rises
like an immense cloud to the cloud
where God is seated,
with a cherub at his side, a great cherub,
a great armed cherub.

Oh, Mapamundi, the grace of every school!
In the chaste schoolroom of my childhood,
when I used to watch the turning
of your round geography,
colored with lemon and caramel,
how helplessly I felt myself condemned,
an offender in a prison tall and dark.

How could I one day tear through
that hermetic cage
the blue seal and come out on the endless sky
where now the stars are music
and the body a light and lazy shadow?

¡Qué miedo insuperable!
Acaso Dios con su bocina ronca,
desde sus barbas de revuelta nieve,
iba a tronar en un gran trueno, justo
como todos sus truenos. O en la roja
atmósfera en que el Diablo precipita
hirviente azufre, hundir al desdichado
—propicio leño a la infernal candela—
que imaginó en su fiebre
romper el equilibrio ponderado
del Mapamundi, gracia de la escuela.

Pero Dios no lo supo,
ni el Diablo se enteró. Titán en vela,
el hombre augusto, el denso
mortal que arde y fornica,
que repta a veces y que a veces vuela,
el hombre soberano y cotidiano
que come, suda, llora, enferma, ríe,
el que te da la mano
en la calle y te dice: "¡Qué buen tiempo!"
o "¡Es duro este verano!" Tu cercano,
tu próximo, tu hermano,
deshizo la clausura,
rompió el sello celeste
que como techo astral del mundo había,
y se lanzó a la noche inmensa y pura.

Llenad la copa del amor, vacía.
Mezclad, mezclemos risas y alcoholes,
sangres, suspiros, huesos,
corazones y besos,
relámpagos y soles.

Suba el terrestre brindis
por la paz, por la vida,
y si queréis, mientras el brindis sube,
recordad que aún reposa sosegado,
recordad que aún reposa
Dios en su inmensa nube,
con un querube al lado, un gran querube,
un gran querube armado.

What insurmountable fear!
Perhaps God with his menacing trumpet,
between his whiskers of turned over snow,
would thunder in a great thunderclap,
as just as all his thunderclaps are. Or in
the scarlet atmosphere in which the Devil casts
boiling sulfur, sink the wretch
—good wood for the infernal fire—
who in his frenzy dreamed of
breaking the carefully conceived balance
of the Mapamundi, the grace of every school.

But God never knew of it,
nor was the Devil informed. A titan
on watch, august man, that obscure
mortal who burns and fornicates,
who sometimes crawls and sometimes flies,
the sovereign and common man
who eats, sweats, cries, gets sick, laughs,
the one who gives you his hand
in the street and says: "What good weather!"
or "This is a hard summer!" Your neighbor,
your relative, your brother,
ended his confinement,
broke the celestial seal
that was the world's astral ceiling,
and launched himself into the pure and immense night.

Fill the, empty, cup of love.
Mix, let's all mix alcohol and laughter,
blood, sighes, bones,
hearts, and kisses,
suns and lightening flashes.

Let the terrestial toast rise
in the name of peace, of life,
and if you wish, while the toast rises,
remember that still resting peacefully,
remember that still resting
God is on his immense cloud,
with a cherub at his side, a great cherub,
a great armed cherub.

1. Canción China a dos voces

Hacia China quisiera partir,
para hablar con el viejo dragón . . .
    ¿Con el viejo dragón?
    Es inútil partir:
    el dragón ha partido en avión.

Una pipa de sueño fumar
y en el humo olvidar mi dolor . . .
    ¿Olvidar tu dolor?
    Es inútil fumar:
    Despertar a la vida es mejor.

¡Oh volver nuevamente, volver
dueño huraño, a mis siembras de arroz!
    ¿A tus siembras de arroz?
    Es inútil volver;
    sembró en ellas el pueblo su voz.

Entre lotos marchitos bogar
y añorar su pasado esplendor . . .
    ¿Su pasado esplendor?
    Es inútil bogar:
    mira el loto: decora un tractor.

2. La canción de Wang Tse-Yu

Ay, cuando Wang Tse-Yu nació,
lunas, amargas lunas antes,
antes
de la gran revolución,
cayó como un pedruzco negro,
pasó como un pequeño perro,
lloró sin cuna y sin pañuelo,
antes, muchas lunas antes,
antes
de la gran revolución.

Hoy he visto a Wang Tse-Yu:
¿Querrás decirme, amigo,
qué estabas haciendo tú,
alto el corazón en punta,

Chinese Songs

1. Chinese Song in Two Voices

To China I would like to go
and speak with the ancient dragon there . . .
> *With the ancient dragon there?*
> *How useless to go:*
> *some time back he fled by air.*

If I could light my pipe of dreams
and in the smoke all pain forget . . .
> *All pain forget?*
> *How useless to smoke:*
> *to face life straight is better yet.*

I yearn to be once more intractable
master of the rice-rich land . . .
> *The rice-rich land?*
> *How useless to yearn:*
> *it's peoples' rice; together they stand.*

Oh, among faded lotus to stroll
mourning for a splendor past . . .
> *A splendor past?*
> *How useless to stroll:*
> *among the lotus, a tractor at last!*

2. Song of Wang Tse-Yu

Oh, when Wang Tse-Yu was born,
moons and bitter moons before,
before
the great Revolution:
he dropped like a black stone,
hung on like a small whelp,
and cried without a cradle or a diaper;
before, many moons before,
before
the great Revolution.

Today I spoke with Wang Tse-Yu:
can you tell me, brother,
what's happened to you—
glorious heart held high,

los negros ojos llenos de luz
y tu gran país labrado
en dura llama y cielo azul?
¿Querras decirme, amigo,
qué estabas haciendo tú?

Gané mi tierra con mi lanza
(me respondió Wang Tse-Yu)
gané mi lanza con mi vida,
gané mi vida con mi sangre,
gané mi sangre con mi sueño . . .
Hoy mi sueño es estar despierto
(me respondió Wang Tse-Yu).

3. La canción del regreso

a Jorge Amado

¿Conoces tú
la tierra del arroz y del bambú?
¿No la conoces tú?

Yo vengo de Pekín.
Pekín
sin mandarín,
ni palanquín.
Yo vengo de Shanghai:
no hay
ni un yanqui ya en Shanghai.

Allá
la vida en flor está.
Se ve
la vida puesta en pie.

¡Canta conmigo, amigo,
y dí como yo digo!
No hay
ni un yanqui ya en Shanghai.
Pekín
enterró al mandarin.
¡Corre a ver tú
la tierra del arroz y del bambú!

black eyes filled with light
from the blue sky and hard passion
of your great land's toil?
Can you tell me, brother,
what's happened to you?

I won my land with my lance
(responded Wang Tse-Yu),
I won my lance with my life,
I won my life with my blood,
I won my blood with my dreams . . .
Today my dream is to be awake
(responded Wang Tse-Yu).

3. Song of Return

for Jorge Amado

Is it clear to you,
the land of rice and of bamboo?
Isn't it clear to you?

I have seen Peking:
Peking,
no mandarin
nor palanquin.
I have seen Shanghai:
I cry,
no more Yankees in Shanghai.
It's awesome
how life's begun to blossom.
It's strange
how life's begun to change.

Sing with me, brother,
and speak as I speak!

I cry,
no more Yankees in Shanghai.
Peking:
the coffin of the mandarin.
Run, behold it . . . you,
the land of rice and of bamboo!

4. El jarrón

En el candor de mi niñez lejana,
entre el libro y el juego,
China era un gran jarro de porcelana
amarilla con un dragón de fuego.

También la familiar y fugitiva
hora de la hortaliza y del tren de lavado,
y Andrés, el cantonés de gramática esquiva,
verde y recién fundado.

Luego fue Sun Yat-sen en la múltiple foto,
con su sueño romántico y roto.

Y por fin noche y día,
la gran marcha tenaz y sombría,
y por fin la victoria y por fin la mañana
y por fin lo que yo no sabía:
toda la sangre que cabía
en un jarrón de porcelana.

5. Primero de Octubre

Pekín, 59

*Coplas a la manera
popular china*

Recuerdo cuando China
era una bestia fina
y endémica. La mano
hambrienta en cada esquina.

Recuerdo cuando era
humo de adormidera.
En un mástil de sangre,
la bandera extranjera.

Recuerdo la sumisa
Corte de la Sonrisa,
y el push-push con el cónsul,
(un cónsul en camisa).

Enciende el pueblo ahora
su lámpara y su aurora.
Arde la calle; es una
gran serpiente sonora.

4. The Vase

In my youth, far off and chaste,
among my books and childhood games,
China meant a porcelain vase,
yellow, with a dragon's flames.

It meant besides, familiar and brief,
vegetable season, wash on the line,
and young Andres a Cantonese—
his speech so newly-learned and shy.

Then a photo of Sun Yat-sen was seen,
with his romantic and shattered dream.

Then at last night turned to day:
the long march, relentless as truth;
then victory and dawn's bright ray.
And finally what I never knew:
the drops and drops of blood that lay
in the porcelain vase of my youth.

5. First of October

Peking, '59

*Verses in the popular
Chinese style*

Ancient China, I repeat,
was a specimen quite sweet;
endemic too, and always with
a begging hand on every street.

Oh, I remember well
opium's burning smell
and the bloody spire tall
where tolled the foreigner's bell.

I have a memory vile:
the Court of the Fawning Smile;
a push-push with the consul,
the consul dressed in style.

Now liberated people hold
burning dawn, a torch of gold;
the street in flames advances
like a serpent great and bold.

41

Trueno de agua marina
alza cantando China:
brazo de sueño y músculo,
márfil y trenza fina.

El estandarte obrero
saluda al limonero;
liban la miel del loto
mariposas de acero.

Wu Sang-Kuei

Wu Sang-Kuei, de tus huesos
no queda más que polvo,
un puñado de polvo en el polvo de China.
Pero en la Gran Muralla, en Chanjaikuán,
entre el viento y las águilas,
hay un lugar maldito,
una puerta de piedra,
la que tú abriste al enemigo Sing.

Wu Sang-Kuei, general y traidor, todavía
tu sucio nombre lleno de moscas
hiede bajo el gran sol del mediodía.

Paul Éluard

Guardo de Paul Éluard
una mirada pura, un rostro grave
y aquella forma entre severa y suave
de hablar.

Con el albor del día fuimos en su busca
y había partido . . .
Fue una partida brusca,
sin *au revoir* ni adiós, sin pañuelo y sin ruido.

¿A dónde fue? ¡Quién sabe!
¡Quién lo podrá saber!
(¡Oh, la mirada pura, el rostro grave
y aquella forma entre severa y suave
de ser!)

In a thunderous, rolling wave
the song of China grows today
of marble fine and tresses pure,
arms for toil, arms for play.

The workers' banner will not yield;
it greets the blossoms of the field.
Nectar of the lotus is drunk
by butterflies of tempered steel!

Wu Sang-Kuei

Of your bones, Wu Sang-Kuei,
nothing but dust remains,
a handful of dust on the dust of China.
But on The Great Wall, in Shanghaikan,
between the wind and the eagles,
there is a heinous place,
a door of stone,
the one you opened to the enemy Sing.

Wu Sang-Kuei, General and traitor,
your name, filthy and full of flies,
still reeks in the high noon sun.

Paul Éluard

I conserve of Paul Éluard
a pristine glance, a grave face
and that manner between soft and severe
of speaking.

With the dawn we went looking for him
and he had left . . .
It was a brusque departure,
without *au revoir* nor good-bye,
without handkerchief nor noise.

Where did he go? Who knows!
Who can possibly know!
(Oh, pristine glance, the grave face
and that manner between soft and severe
of being!)

Mi chiquita

La chiquita que yo tengo
tan negra como é,
no la cambio po ninguna,
po ninguna otra mujé.

Ella laba, plancha, cose,
y sobre tó, caballero,
¡como cosina!

Si la bienen a bucá
pa bailá,
pa comé,
ella me tiene que llebá,
o traé.

Ella dice: mi santo,
tú no me puede dejá;
bucamé,
bucamé,
bucamé,
pa gosá.

Piedra de horno

La tarde abandonada
gime deshecha en lluvia.
Del cielo caen recuerdos
y entran por la ventana.
Duros suspiros rotos,
quimeras calcinadas.
Lentamente va viniendo tu cuerpo.
Llegan tus manos en su órbita
de aguardiente de caña;
tus pies inagotables quemados por la danza,
y tus muslos, tenazas del espasmo,
y tu boca, sustancia
comestible, y tu cintura
de abierto caramelo.

Llegan tus brazos de oro, tus dientes sanguinarios;
de pronto entran tus ojos traicionados,
tu piel tendida, preparada
para la siesta;

44

My Little Woman

Black as she is,
I wouldn't trade
the woman I got
for no other woman.

She wash, iron, sew,
and, man,
can that woman cook!

If they want her
to go dancing
or go eat,
she got to take me,
she got to bring me back.

She say: "Daddy,
you can't leave me 't all,
come get me,
come get me,
come get me,
let's have a ball."

Ovenstone

The abandoned evening
moans, undone by rain.
Memories fall from the sky
and slip through my window.
Heavy, broken sighs,
chimeras burned to ashes.
Slowly, slowly, you appear:
hands in their
cane-liquor orbit,
tireless, dance-burned feet,
your thighs, tongs for spasm,
and your mouth, an edible
fruit, and your waist
of generous caramel.

Then, golden arms, bloodthirsty teeth,
and suddenly your betrayed eyes;
next your washed skin, prepared
for the siesta;

tu olor a selva repentina; tu garganta
gritando (no sé, me lo imagino), gimiendo
(no sé, me lo figuro), quejándose (no sé, supongo, creo);
tu garganta profunda
retorciendo palabras prohibidas.

Un rio de promesas
baja de tus cabellos,
se demora en tus senos,
cuaja al fin en un charco de melaza en tu vientre,
viola tu carne firme de noturno secreto.

Carbón ardiendo y piedra de horno
en esta tarde fria de lluvia y de silencio.

Ana María

Ana María,
la trenza que te cae
sobre el pecho, me mira
con ojos de serpiente
desde su piel torcida.
Yo entre todas tus gracias
señalo la sonrisa
con que al arder escondes
la llama de ti misma.

Es cuando te recorren
las nubes pensativas
y en tu cuerpo metálico
la tempestad se estira
como una lenta y suave
serpiente suspendida . . .

Deportes

¿Qué sé yo de boxeo,
yo, que confundo el *jab* con el *upper cut?*
Y sin embargo, a veces
sube desde mi infancia
como una nube inmensa desde el fondo de un valle,

a sudden jungle-smell, your throat
calling (I don't know, I imagine), moaning
(I don't know, I think), complaining (I don't know, I
suppose, I believe)
. . . your deep throat
twisting out forbidden words.

A river of promises
falls from your hair,
lingers at your breasts,
then thickens in a pool of molasses on your belly
and violates the firm flesh of nocturnal secrets.

Burning coals and ovenstones
on this cold evening of rain and silence.

Ana María

Ana María,
the braid that falls
upon your breast is watching
me with serpent eyes
from its twisted skin.
Among your many charms
I choose the smile
with which you veil
the flame that burns inside.

It's when thought-laden clouds
within you stir,
and your metallic
body's storm expires
like the slow, smooth, shudder
of a serpent . . .

Sports

What do I know of boxing,
who can't tell a jab from an uppercut?
But all the same, at times,
up from my boyhood
like a great cloud from the depths of a valley,

sube, me llega Johnson,
el negro montañoso
el *dandy* atlético magnético de betún.
Es un aparecido familiar,
melón redondo y cráneo,
sonrisa de abanico de plumas
y la azucena prohibida
que hacía rabiar a Lynch.

O bien, si no, percibo un rayo de la gloria
de Wills y Carpentier; o de la gloria
de Sam Langford . . . Gloria de cuando ellos
piafaban en sus guantes, relinchaban,
altos los puros cuellos,
húmedo el ojo casto
y la feroz manera
de retozar en un pasto
de soga y de madera.

Mas sobre todo, pienso
en Kid Charol, el gran rey sin corona,
y en Chocolate, el gran rey coronado,
y en Black Bill, con sus nervios de goma.
Yo, que confundo al *jab* con el *upper cut,*
canto el cuero, los guantes,
el *ring* . . . Busco palabras,
las robo a los cronistas deportivos
y grito entonces: Salud, músculo y sangre,
victoria vuestra y nuestra!
Heroes también, titanes.
Sus peleas
fueron como claros poemas.
¿Pensáis tal vez que yo no puedo decir tanto,
porque confundo el *jab* con el *upper cut?*
¿Pensáis que yo exagero?
Junto a los yanquis y el francés,
los míos, mis campeones,
de amargos puños y sólidos pies,
son sus iguales, son
como espejos que el tiempo no empaña,
mástiles másculos donde también ondea
muestra bandera al fúlgido y álgido viento que sopla en
    la montaña!

it comes—I see Johnson,
the mountainous Black,
the athletic, magnetic, bituminous dandy.
It's a familiar vision
of melon-round cranium,
feathered-fan smile,
and the forbidden white lily
that drove Lynch wild.

Or if not that, I sometimes spy the flame of glory
lighting Wills and Carpentier; or the glory
of Sam Langford: glory of when they
pawed with their gloves, neighed,
and honest eyes gleaming,
fine necks held high,
romped in fierce
style through pastures
of ropes and wood.

But most of all I think
of Kid Charol, the great king uncrowned;
of Chocolate, the great king crowned;
and Black Bill, with tendons of elastic.
I, who can't tell a jab from an uppercut,
sing of leather, gloves,
the ring. I seek words,
rob them from the sports page,
and shout, "Hurrah for blood and muscle,
for a triumph yours and ours!
Heroes, Titans,
your fights were like
fine poems."
You think perhaps I shouldn't say so much,
because I can't tell a jab from an uppercut?
You think I stretch the truth?
Well, next to the Yankees and the Frenchman,
mine, my champions
of bitter fists and solid stance
walk tall, are
mirrors that the years can't cloud, are
virile staffs where also waves our banner
in the clear, cold wind that sighs through the mountains.

¿Qué sé yo de ajedrez?
Nunca moví un alfil, un peón.
Tengo los ojos ciegos
para el álgebra, los caracteres griegos
y ese tablero filosófico
donde cada figura es
una interrogación.
Pero recuerdo a Capablanca, me lo recuerdan.
En los caminos
me asaltan voces como lanzas.

—Tú, que vienes de Cuba ¿no has visto a Capablanca?
(Yo respondo que Cuba
se hunde en los ríos como un cocodrilo verde.)

—Tú, que vienes de Cuba, ¿cómo era Capablanca?
(Yo respondo que Cuba
vuela en la tarde como una paloma triste.)

—Tú, que vienes de Cuba, ¿no vendrá Capablanca?
(Yo respondo que Cuba
suena en la noche como una guitarra sola.)

—Tú, que vienes de Cuba, ¿dónde está Capablanca?
(Yo respondo que Cuba es una lágrima.)

        Pero las voces me vigilan,
        me tienden trampas, me rodean
        y me acuchillan y desangran;
        pero las voces se levantan
        como unas duras, finas bardas;
        pero las voces se deslizan
        como sepientes largas, húmedas;
        pero las voces me persiguen
        como alas . . .

Asi pues Capablanca
no está en su trono, sino que anda,
camina, ejerce su gobierno
en las calles del mundo.

What do I know of chess,
who never moved a bishop or a pawn?
My eyes are blind
to the algebra, the strange signs,
and that philosophical board
where every piece
is a question mark.
But I remember Capablanca; they remind me of him.
As I pass
voices assault me like a lance.

     "You, who come from Cuba, have you seen
     Capablanca?"
(I respond that Cuba
is a green crocodile, submerged in the river.)

     "You, who come from Cuba, what was
     Capablanca like?"
(I respond that Cuba
is a sad dove, soaring at evening.)

     "You, who come from Cuba, do you think
     Capablanca will visit?"
(I respond that Cuba
is a lonely guitar, dreaming at night.)

     "You, who come from Cuba, where is
     Capablanca?"
(I respond that Cuba is a tear.)

     But the voices lie in wait,
     trick me, surround me,
     knife me, and bleed me;
     but the voices rise
     like stubborn, slender oaks;
     but the voices slither
     like long, moist serpents;
     but the voices pursue me
     like wings . . .

In this way, Capablanca
has no throne, but walks,
parades, and reigns
in the streets of all the world.

Bien está que nos lleve
de Noruega a Zanzíbar,
de Cáncer a la nieve.
Va en un caballo blanco,
caracoleando
sobre puentes y ríos,
junto a torres y alfiles,
el sombrero en la mano
(para las damas)
la sonrisa en el aire
(para los caballeros)
y su caballo blanco
sacando chispas puras
del empedrado . . .

**Pequeña oda a un
negro boxeador
cubano**

Tus guantes
puestos en la punta de tu cuerpo de ardilla,
y el *punch* de tu sonrisa.

El Norte es fiero y rudo, boxeador.
Ese mismo Broadway,
que en actitud de vena se desangra
para chillar junto a los *rings*
en que tú saltas como un moderno mono elástico,
sin el resorte de las sogas,
ni los almohadones del *clinch;*
ese mismo Broadway,
que unta de asombro su boca de melón
ante tus puños explosivos
y tus actuales zapatos de charol;
ese mismo Broadway,
es el que estira su hocico con una enorme lengua húmeda,
para lamer glotonamente
toda la sangre de nuestro cañaveral.

De seguro que tú
no vivirás al tanto de ciertas cosas nuestras,
ni de ciertas cosas de allá,
porque el *training* es duro y el músculo traidor,
y hay que estar hecho un toro,
como dices alegremente, para que el golpe duela más.

How well he leads us
from Norway to Zanzibar,
from Cancer to the snows.
Borne by a white steed,
among bishops and castles,
his hat in the air
(for the ladies)
and a smile on his face
(for the gentlemen),
he caracoles
at bridges over rivers,
his white steed
striking fine sparks
on the highway!

Small Ode to a Black Cuban Boxer

Your gloves
cocked before a squirrel-quick body
and the punch in your smile!

Boxer, the North is hard and cruel.
The very Broadway
that like a vein bleeds out
to scream beside the ring
wherein you bound, a brand new rubber monkey,
without resorting to the ropes
or the cushions of a clinch . . .
the very Broadway
that oils its melon-mouth with fear
before your fists of dynamite
and stylish patent leather shoes . . .
is the same Broadway
that stretches out its snout, its moist enormous tongue,
to lick and glut upon
our canefields' vital blood!

It's clear
you're not aware of certain things down here,
nor of certain things up there;
for training is tough, muscle a traitor,
and one must gain—you say with joy
—a bull-like strength, to make the punch hurt more.

Tu inglés,
un poco más precario que tu endeble español,
sólo te ha de servir para entender sobre la lona
cuanto en su verde slang
mascan las mandíbulas de los que tú derrumbas
jab a *jab*.

En realidad acaso no necesites otra cosa,
porque como seguramente pensarás.
ya tienes tu lugar.

Es bueno, al fin y al cabo,
hallar un *punching bag*,
eliminar la grasa bajo el sol.
saltar,
sudar,
nadar,
y de la suiza al *shadow boxing,*
de la ducha al comedor,
salir pulido, fino, fuerte
como un bastón recién labrado
con agresividades de *black jack*.

Y ahora que Europa se desnuda
para tostar su carne al sol
y busca en Harlem y en La Habana
jazz y son
lucirse negro mientras aplaude el bulevar,
y frente a la envidia de los blancos
hablar en negro de verdad.

¿Qué color?

*Su piel era negra, pero
con el alma purísima
como la nieve
blanca . . .*

Evtuchenko (según el
cable), ante el asesinato
de Lutero King

Qué alma tan blanca, dicen,
la de aquel noble pastor.
Su piel tan negra, dicen,
su piel tan negra de color,
era por dentro nieve,
azucena,
leche fresca,
algodón.
Qué candor.
No había ni una mancha
en su blanquísimo interior.

54

Your English,
only a bit more shaky than your feeble Spanish,
is good enough inside the ring
for you to understand that filthy slang
spit from the jaws of those you waste
jab by jab.

In truth, perhaps that's all you need.
And, as you certainly will think,
you've got it made.

For after all, it's great
to find a punching bag,
work off some fat beneath the sun—
to leap,
to sweat,
to swim—
and from shadow-boxing to a fight,
from the shower to the table,
come out polished, fine, and strong,
like a newly-crafted cane
with the agressiveness of a black jack.

So now that Europe strips itself
to brown its hide beneath the sun
and seeks in Harlem and Havana
jazz and *son:*
the Negro reigns while boulevards applaud!
Let the envy of the whites
know proud, authentic black!

What Color?

His skin was black,
but with the purest soul,
white as the snow . . .

Yevtushenko (in a
cable), on the assassina-
tion of Martin Luther
King

Such a white soul, they say,
that noble pastor had.
His skin so black, they say,
his skin so black in color,
was on the inside snow,
a white lily,
fresh milk,
cotton.
Such innocence.
There wasn't one stain
on his impeccable interior.

55

(En fin, valiente hallazgo:
"El negro que tenía el alma blanca,"
aquel novelón.)

Pero podría decirse de otro modo:
Qué alma tan poderosa negra
la del dulcísimo pastor.
Qué alta pasión negra
ardía en su ancho corazón.
Qué pensamientos puros negros
su grávido cerebro alimentó.
Qué negro amor,
tan repartido
sin color.

¿Por qué no,
por qué no iba a tener el alma negra
aquel heroico pastor?

Negra como el carbón.

Gobernador

Cuando hayas enseñado tu perro
a abalanzarse sobre un negro
y arrancarle el hígado de un bocado,
cuando también tú sepas
por lo menos ladrar y menear el rabo,
alégrate, ya puedes
¡oh blanco!
ser gobernador de tu Estado.

Escolares

Cumplieron sus tareas (prácticas) los escolarizados
muchachos blancos de Alabama:
cada uno presentó una rama
de flamboyant, con cinco negros ahorcados.

(In short, a handsome find:
"The Black whose soul was white,"
that curiosity).

Still it might be said another way:
What a powerful black soul
that gentlest of pastors had.
What proud black passion
burned in his open heart.
What pure black thoughts
were nourished in his fertile brain.
What black love,
so colorlessly
given.

And why not,
why couldn't that heroic pastor
have a soul that's black?

A soul as black as coal.

The Governor

When you've trained your dog just right
to pounce upon a defenseless Black
and tear his liver out with a bite;
when you yourself are part of the pack,
and wag your tail and howl at night . . .
you qualify, white man filled with hate,
to run for governor of your state!

Schoolwork

White kids prepare, in Alabama today,
as practical homework, when the books are read,
flamboyant in a lovely bouquet,
with five black corpses hanging dead.

Little Rock

A Enrique Amorim

Un *blue* llora con lágrimas de música
en la mañana fina.
El Sur blanco sacude
su látigo y golpea. Van los niños
negros entre fusiles pedagógicos
a su escuela de miedo.
Cuando a sus aulas lleguen,
Jim Crow será el maestro,
hijos de Lynch serán sus condiscípulos
y habrá en cada pupitre
de cada niño negro,
tinta de sangre, lápices de fuego.

Así es el Sur. Su látigo no cesa.

En aquel mundo faubus,
bajo aquel duro cielo faubus de gangrena,
los niños negros pueden
no ir junto a los blancos a la escuela.
O bien quedarse suavemente en casa.
O bien (nunca se sabe)
dejarse golpear hasta el martirio.
O bien no aventurarse por las calles.
O bien morir a bala y a saliva.
O no silbar al paso de una muchacha blanca.
O en fin, bajar los ojos yes,
doblar el cuerpo yes,
arrodillarse yes,
en aquel mundo libre yes
de que habla Foster Tonto en aeropuerto y aeropuerto
mientras la pelotilla blanca,
una graciosa pelotilla blanca,
presidencial, de golf, como un planeta mínimo,
rueda en el césped puro, terso, fino,
verde, casto, tierno, suave, yes.

Y bien, ahora,
señoras y señores, señoritas,
ahora niños,
ahora viejos peludos y pelados,
ahora indios, mulatos, negros, zambos,
ahora pensad lo que sería
el mundo todo Sur,
el mundo todo sangre y todo látigo,

Little Rock

For Enrique Amorim

A blues cries tears of music
in the clear morning air.
White South draws its lash and strikes.
Little black children pass through pedagogical rifles
to their school of terror.
Once inside the classroom
Jim Crow will be their teacher,
sons of Lynch their playmates;
and there will at every desk
of every child that's black
bloody ink and flaming pens.

This is the South, the never-ending curse of South!

In that Faubus-world,
beneath the hard Faubus-sky of gangrene,
a black child is free:
    not to be in school among the whites,
to stay peacefully at home,
    not to walk out in the streets,
to be martyred by beatings,
    not to whistle at a white woman,
to be killed by spit and lead,
        and even to lower his head . . . *yes,*
        bend his back . . . *yes,*
        fall to his knees . . . *yes,*
        in that free world . . . *yes,*
of which John Foster Stupid speaks from airport to
    airport:
while that tiny white ball,
that pretty, tiny, white, presidential ball
(golf) rolls like the smallest of planets
over fine, stiff, clean, chaste, tender,
sweet, green grass . . . *yes!*

Now then, ladies,
gentlemen, girls,
old men, rich men, poor men,
Indians, Mulattoes, Negroes, Zambos,
think what it would be:
a world all South,
a world all blood and lash,

el mundo todo escuela de blancos para blancos,
el mundo todo Rock y todo Little,
el munco todo yanqui, todo Faubus . . .

                    Pensad por un momento,
imaginadlo un solo instante.

Mau-Maus   Envenenada tinta
habla de los mau-maus;
negros de diente y uña,
de antropofagia y totem.
Gruñe la tinta, cuenta,
dice que los mau-maus
mataron a un inglés . . .
(Aquí en secreto: era
el mismo inglés de kepis
profanador, de rifle
civilizado y remington,
que en el pulmón de Africa
con golpe seco y firme
clavó su daga-imperio,
de hierro abecedario,
de sífilis, de pólvora,
de *money, business, yes.*)

Letras de larga tinta
cuentan que los mau-maus
casas de sueño y trópico
británicas tomaron
y a fuego, sangre, muerte,
bajo el asalto bárbaro
cien ingleses cayeron . . .
(Aquí en secreto: eran
los mismos cien ingleses
a quienes Londres dijo:
—Matad, comed mau-maus;
barred, incendiad Kenya;
que ni un solo kikuyus
viva y que sus mujeres
por siempre de ceniza
servida vean su mesa
y seco vean su vientre.)

a world of white schools for whites,
a world all Rock and all Little,
a world all Yankee and all Faubus . . .

      Consider that a moment.
Imagine for just one instant!

Mau-Maus

Poisoned ink
speaks of the Mau-Maus:
anthropophagous Blacks of tooth
and nail and totem.
Ink grunts and speaks
and says the Mau-Maus
killed an Englishman . . .
(Just between us: it was
a desecrator, shako-Englishman,
his rifle civilized
and Remington,
whose dry, decisive thrust
pierced the lung of Africa
with an Empire-dagger of
alphabetizing steel . . .
of syphilis, gunpowder,
money, business, yes.)

Tall type tells
that Mau-Maus
took British houses
of tropical dream
and in fire, blood, and death,
in a barbarous assault,
one-hundred English died . . .
(Just between us: they were
the same one-hundred English
London told,
"Kill and eat the Mau-Maus;
burn and clean up Kenya.
Leave not a single Kikuyu alive
and may their women
ever see the table
spread with ashes;
may they feel their wombs forever dry.")

Tinta de largas letras
cuenta que los mau-maus
arrasan como un río
salvaje las cosechas,
envenenan las aguas,
queman las tierras próvidas,
matan toros y ciervos.
(Aquí en secreto: eran
dueños de diez mil chozas,
del árbol, de la lluvia,
del sol, de la montaña,
dueños de la semilla,
del surco, de la nube,
del viento, de la paz . . .)

Algo sencillo y simple
¡oh inglés de duro kepis!,
simple y sencillo: dueños.

Calor

El calor raja la noche.
La noche cae tostada
sobre el rio.

¡Qué grito,
qué grito fresco en las aguas
el grito que da la noche
quemada!

Rojo calor para negros.
¡Tambor!
Calor para torsos fúlgidos.
¡Tambor!
Calor con lenguas de fuego
sobre espinazos desnudos . . .
¡Tambor!

El agua de las estrellas
empapa los cocoteros
despiertos.
¡Tambor!

And tall type tells
that Mau-Maus
wipe out harvests
like a savage river,
poison waters,
burn productive lands,
and slaughter steers and deer.
(Just between us: they were
owners of ten-thousand huts,
of trees and rain,
of sun and mountains;
owners of the seed,
the furrows, clouds,
the wind, and peace . . .)

Something plain and simple—
Oh, implacable shako-English!
—plain and simple
                    . . . owners.

Heat

Heat splits the night.
Night falls toasted
on the river.

What cry,
what fresh cry in the waters,
the cry of burning night!

Red heat for Blacks.
Drum!
Heat for darkened torsos.
Drum!
Heat with tongues of fire
on naked spines . . .
Drum!

Water from the stars
soaks awakened
coco-palms.
Drum!

Alta luz de las estrellas.
¡Tambor!
El faro polar vacila . . .
¡Tambor!

¡Fuego a bordo! ¡Fuego a bordo!
¡Tambor!
¿Es cierto? ¡Huid! ¡Es mentira!
¡Tambor!
Costas sordas, cielos sordos . . .
¡Tambor!

Las islas van navegando,
navegando, navegando,
van navegando encendidas.

Ancestros

Por lo que dices, Fabio,
un arcángel tu abuelo fue con sus esclavos.
Mi abuelo, en cambio,
fue un diablo con sus amos.
El tuyo murió de un garrotazo.
Al mío, lo colgaron.

**Un negro canta en
Nueva York**

Una paloma me dijo
que anduvo por Nueva York:
volando anduvo,
pero no vio
ni una estrella ni una flor.
    Piedra y humo
    y humo y plomo
    y plomo y llama
y llama y piedra y plomo y humo
siempre halló.

—Paloma ¿y usted no vio
a un negro llorando?
                —No.
—¿El negro cantaba?
                —Sí.

Bright starlight.
Drum!
The pole star glitters . . .
Drum!

Fire on board! Fire on board!
Drum!
Is it true? Run! It's a lie!
Drum!
Mute coasts, mute skies . . .
Drum!

The islands sailing,
sailing, sailing,
sailing wrapped in flames.

Ancestry

Fabio, from what you say,
your grandpa was an archangel with his slaves.
My grandpa, on the other hand,
was a demon with his masters.
Yours died cudgeled.
Mine they hanged.

**A Negro Sings in
New York City**

A dove told me
it passed through New York City:
it passed through flying
but did not see
a single flower, a single star.
      Rock and smoke
        and smoke and lead
        and lead and flame
and flame and rock and lead and smoke again.

"Dove, and you didn't see
a Negro crying?"
          "No."
"Did the Negro sing?"
            "Yes."

Cuando lo ví,
me saludó.
Cantó,
siguió cantando así:

—Tengo un pedazo de sueño,
paloma,
que un soñador me dejó;
con ese sueño, paloma,
voy hacer yo
una estrella y una flor.
(La estrella y su resplandor.
El resplandor en la flor).

—Tengo un pedazo de canto,
paloma,
que un cantador me dejó;
con ese canto, paloma,
voy hacer yo
un himno y una canción.
(El himno contra Jim Crow.
De paz y paz la canción).

—Tengo un pedazo de hierro,
paloma,
que un herrero me dejó;
con ese hierro, paloma,
voy hacer yo
un martillo y una hoz.
(¡Doy con el martillo, doy!
¡Corto y corto con la hoz!).

**Balada de los dos
abuelos**

Sombras que sólo yo veo,
me escoltan mis dos abuelos.
Lanza con punta de hueso,
tambor de cuero y madera:
mi abuelo negro.
Gorguera en el cuello ancho,
gris armadura guerrera:
mi abuelo blanco.

I saw him,
he greeted me.
He sang,
and went on singing:

'Dove, I have a piece of dream,
a dreamer left to me;
Dove, with that dream
I plan to make
a star and a flower.
(The star with its radiance.
The radiance in the flower)

'Dove, I have a piece of verse,
a poet left to me;
Dove, with that verse
I plan to make
a hymn and a song.
(The hymn against Jim Crow.
The song of peace and peace again.)

'Dove, I have a piece of steel,
a Blacksmith left to me;
Dove, with that steel
I plan to make a hammer and a sickle.
(I'll strike with the hammer, strike!
Cut with the sickle, cut!)

**Ballad of the two
Grandfathers**

Shadows which only I see,
I'm watched by my two grandfathers.
A bone-point lance,
a drum of hide and wood:
my black grandfather.
A ruff on a broad neck,
a warrior's gray armament:
my white grandfather.

Africa de selvas húmedas
y de gordos gongos sordos . . .
—¡Me muero!
(Dice mi abuelo negro).
Aguaprieta de caimanes,
verdes mañanas de cocos . . .
—¡Me canso!
(Dice mi abuelo blanco).
Oh velas de amargo viento,
galeón ardiendo en oro . . .
—¡Me muero!
(Dice mi abuelo negro).
¡Oh costas de cuello virgen
engañadas de abalorios . . . !
—¡Me canso!
(Dice mi abuelo blanco).
¡Oh puro sol repujado,
preso en el aro del trópico;
oh luna redonda y limpia
sobre el sueño de los monos!

¡Qué de barcos, qué de barcos!
¡Qué de negros, qué de negros!
¡Qué largo fulgor de cañas!
¡Qué látigo el del negrero!
Piedra de llanto y de sangre,
venas y ojos entreabiertos,
y madrugadas vacías,
y atardeceres de ingenio,
y una gran voz, fuerte voz,
despedazando ei silencio.
¡Qué de barcos, qué de barcos,
qué de negros!

Sombras que sólo yo veo,
me escoltan mis dos abuelos.

Don Federico me grita
y Taita Facundo calla;
los dos en la noche sueñan
y andan, andan.
Yo los junto.
            —¡Federico!
¡Facundo! Los dos se abrazan.

Africa's humid jungles
with thick and muted gongs . . .
"I'm dying!"
(My black grandfather says).
Waters dark with alligators,
mornings green with coconuts . . .
"I'm tired!"
(My white grandfather says).
Oh sails of a bitter wind,
galleon burning for gold . . .
"I'm dying"
(My black grandfather says).
Oh coasts with virgin necks
deceived with beads of glass . . . !
"I'm tired!"
(My white grandfather says).
Oh pure and burnished sun,
imprisoned in the tropic's ring;
Oh clear and rounded moon
above the sleep of monkeys!

So many ships, so many ships!
So many Blacks, so many Blacks!
So much resplendent cane!
How harsh the trader's whip!
A rock of tears and blood,
of veins and eyes half-open,
of empty dawns
and plantation sunsets,
and a great voice, a strong voice,
splitting the silence.
So many ships, so many ships,
so many Blacks!

Shadows which only I see,
I'm watched by my two grandfathers.

Don Federico yells at me
and Taita Facundo is silent;
both dreaming in the night
and walking, walking.
I bring them together.
                              "Federico!
Facundo!" They embrace. They sigh,

Los dos suspiran. Los dos
las fuertes cabezas alzan;
los dos del mismo tamaño,
bajo las estrellas altas;
los dos del mismo tamaño,
ansia negra y ansia blanca,
los dos del mismo tamaño,
gritan, sueñan, lloran, cantan.
Sueñan, lloran, cantan.
Lloran, cantan.
¡Cantan!

**Un son para niños
antillanos**

Por el Mar de las Antillas
anda un barco de papel:
anda y anda el barco barco,
sin timonel.

De La Habana a Portobelo,
de Jamaica a Trinidad,
anda y anda el barco barco,
sin capitán.

Una negra va en la popa,
va en la proa un español:
anda y anda el barco barco,
con ellos dos.

Pasan islas, islas, islas,
muchas islas, siempre más;
anda y anda el barco barco,
sin descansar.

Un cañón de chocolate
contra el barco disparó,
y un cañón de azúcar, zúcar,
le contestó.

¡Ay, mi barco marinero,
con un casco de papel!
¡Ay, mi barco negro y blanco
sin timonel!

they raise their sturdy heads;
both of equal size,
beneath the high stars;
both of equal size,
a Black longing, a White longing,
both of equal size,
they scream, dream, weep, sing.
They dream, weep, sing.
They weep, sing.
Sing!

Son for Antillian Children

On the sea of the Antilles
there sails a ship of paper:
the ship ship sailing sailing,
with no helmsman.

Havana to Portobelo,
Jamaica to Trinidad,
the ship ship sailing sailing,
with no captain.

A black woman's in the stern,
a Spaniard's in the prow:
the ship ship sailing sailing,
with them both aboard.

They pass islands, islands, islands,
many islands, always more;
the ship ship sailing sailing,
without rest.

A chocolate cannon fired
a shot against the ship,
and a sugar cannon, sugar,
gave reply.

Oh, my ocean going vessel,
with its little paper hull!
Oh, my ship that's black and white
without a helmsman!

Allá va la negra negra,
junto junto al español;
anda y anda el barco barco
con ellos dos.

El apellido   **I**

Elegía familiar   Desde la escuela
                                   y aún antes . . . Desde el alba, cuando apenas
                                   era una brizna yo de sueño y llanto,
                                   desde entonces,
                                   me dijeron mi nombre. Un santo y seña
                                   para poder hablar con las estrellas.
                                   Tú te llamas, te llamarás . . .
                                   Y luego me entregaron
                                   esto que veis escrito en mi tarjeta,
                                   esto que pongo al pie de mis poemas:
                                   las trece letras
                                   que llevo a cuestas por la calle,
                                   que siempre van conmigo a todas partes.
                                   ¿Es mi nombre, estáis ciertos?
                                   ¿Tenéis todas mis señas?
                                   ¿Ya conocéis mi sangre navegable,
                                   mi geografía llena de oscuros montes,
                                   de hondos y amargos valles
                                   que no están en los mapas?
                                   ¿Acaso visitásteis mis abismos,
                                   mis galerías subterráneas
                                   con grandes piedras húmedas,
                                   islas sobresaliendo en negras charcas
                                   y donde un puro chorro
                                   siento de antiguas aguas
                                   caer desde mi alto corazón
                                   con fresco y hondo estrépito
                                   en un lugar lleno de ardientes árboles,
                                   monos equilibristas,
                                   loros legisladores y culebras?
                                   ¿Toda mi piel (debí decir)
                                   toda mi piel viene de aquella estatua
                                   de mármol español? ¿También mi voz de espanto,
                                   el duro grito de mi garganta? ¿Vienen de allá

72

There you'll find the black black woman,
alongside side of the Spaniard;
the ship ship sailing sailing
with them both aboard.

My Last Name   I

A family elegy   Ever since school
                                    and even before . . . Since the dawn, when I was
                                    barely a patch of sleep and wailing,
                                    since then
                                    I have been told my name. A password
                                    that I might speak with stars.
                                    Your name is, you shall be called . . .
                                    And then they handed me
                                    this you see here written on my card,
                                    this I put at the foot of all poems:
                                    thirteen letters
                                    that I carry on my shoulders through the street,
                                    that are with me always, no matter where I go.
                                    Are you sure it is my name?
                                    Have you got all my particulars?
                                    Do you already know my navigable blood,
                                    my geography full of dark mountains,
                                    of deep and bitter valleys
                                    that are not on the maps?
                                    Perhaps you have visited my chasms,
                                    my subterranean galleries
                                    with great moist rocks,
                                    islands jutting out of black puddles,
                                    where I feel the pure rush
                                    of ancient waters
                                    falling from my proud heart
                                    with a sound that's fresh and deep
                                    to a place of flaming trees,
                                    acrobatic monkeys,
                                    legislative parrots and snakes?
                                    Does all my skin (I should have said),
                                    Does all my skin come from that Spanish marble?
                                    My frightening voice too,
                                    the harsh cry in my throat?

todos mis huesos? ¿Mis raíces y las raíces
de mis raíces y además
estas ramas oscuras movidas por los sueños
y estas flores abiertas en mi frente
y esta savia que amarga mi corteza?
¿Estáis seguros?
¿No hay nada más que eso que habéis escrito,
que eso que habéis sellado
con un sello de cólera?
(¡Oh, debí haber preguntado!).

Y bien, ahora os pregunto:
¿no veis estos tambores en mis ojos?
¿No veis estos tambores tensos y golpeados
con dos lágrimas secas?
¿No tengo acaso
un abuelo nocturno
con una gran marca negra
(más negra todavía que la piel)
una gran marca hecha de un latigazo?
¿No tengo pues
un abuelo mandinga, congo, dahomeyano?
¿Cómo se llama? ¡Oh, sí decídmelo!
¿Andrés? ¿Francisco? ¿Amable?
¿Cómo decís Andrés en congo?
¿Cómo habéis dicho siempre
Francisco en dahomeyano?
En mandinga ¿cómo se dice Amable?
¿O no? ¿Eran, pues, otros nombres?
¡El apellido, entonces!
¿Sabéis mi otro apellido, el que me viene
de aquella tierra enorme, el apellido
sangriento y capturado, que pasó sobre el mar
entre cadenas, que pasó entre cadenas sobre el mar?

¡Ah, no podéis recordarlo!
Lo habéis disuelto en tinta inmemorial.
Lo habéis robado a un pobre negro indefenso.
Los escondisteis, creyendo
que iba a bajar los ojos yo de la vergüenza.
¡Gracias!
¡Os lo agradezco!
¡Gentiles gentes, thank you!

Are all my bones from there?
My roots and the roots
of my roots and also
these dark branches swayed by dreams
and these flowers blooming on my forehead
and this sap embittering my bark?
Are you certain?
Is there nothing more than this that you have written,
than this which you have stamped
with the seal of anger?
(Oh, I should have asked!)

Well then, I ask you now:
Don't you see these drums in my eyes?
Don't you see these drums, tightened and
beaten with two dried-up tears?
Don't I have, perhaps,
a nocturnal grandfather
with a great black scar
(darker still than his skin)
a great scar made by a whip?
Have I not, then,
a grandfather who's Mandingo, Dahoman, Congolese?
What is his name? Oh, yes, give me his name!
Andrés? Francisco? Amable?
How do you say Andrés in Congolese?
How have you always said
Francisco in Dahoman?
In Mandingo, how do you say Amable?
No? Were they, then, other names?
The last name then!
Do you know my other last name, the one that comes
to me from that enormous land, the captured,
bloody last name, that came across the sea
in chains, which came in chains across the sea.

Ah, you can't remember it!
You have dissolved it in immemorial ink.
You stole it from a poor, defenseless Black.
You hid it, thinking that I would
lower my eyes in shame.
Thank you!
I am grateful to you!
Noble people, thanks!

Merci!
Merci bien!
Merci beaucoup!
Pero no . . . ¿Podéis creerlo? No.
Yo estoy limpio.
Brilla mi voz como un metal recién pulido.
Mirad mi escudo: tiene un baobab,
tiene un rinoceronte y una lanza.
Yo soy también el nieto,
biznieto,
tataranieto de un esclavo.
(Que se avergüence el amo).
¿Seré Yelofe?
¿Nicolás Yelofe, acaso?
¿O Nicolás Bakongo?
¿Tal vez Guillén Banguila?
¿O Kumbá?
¿Quizá Guillén Kumbá?
¿O Kongué?
¿Pudiera ser Guillén Kongué?
¡Oh, quién lo sabe!
¡Qué enigma entre las aguas!

II

Siento la noche inmensa gravitar
sobre profundas bestias,
sobre inocentes almas castigadas;
pero también sobre voces en punta,
que despojan al cielo de sus soles,
los más duros,
para condecorar la sangre combatiente.
De algún país ardiente, perforado
por la gran flecha ecuatorial,
sé que vendrán lejanos primos,
remota angustia mía disparada en el viento;
sé que vendrán pedazos de mis venas,
sangre remota mía,
con duro pie aplastando las hierbas asustadas;
sé que vendrán hombres de vidas verdes,
remota selva mía,
con su dolor abierto en cruz y el pecho rojo en llamas.

Merci!
Merci bien!
Merci beaucoup!
But no . . . Can you believe it? No.
I am clean.
My voice sparkles like newly polished metal.
Look at my shield: it has a baobab,
it has a rhinoceros and a spear.
I am also the grandson,
great grandson,
great great grandson of a slave.
(Let the master be ashamed.)
Am I Yelofe?
Nicolás Yelofe, perhaps?
Or Nicolás Bakongo?
Maybe Guillén Banguila?
Or Kumbá?
Perhaps Guillén Kumbá?
Or Kongué?
Could I be Guillén Kongué?
Oh, who knows!
What a riddle in the waters!

II

I feel immense night fall
on profound beasts,
on innocent castigated souls;
but also on ready voices,
which steal suns from the sky,
the brightest suns,
to decorate combatant blood.
From some flaming land pierced through
by the great equatorial arrow,
I know there will come distant cousins,
my ancestral anguish cast upon the winds;
I know there will come portions of my veins,
my ancestral blood,
with calloused feet bending frightened grasses;
I know there will come men whose lives are green,
my ancestral jungle,
with their pain open like a cross and their breasts red
    with flames.

Sin conocernos nos reconoceremos en el hambre,
en la tuberculosis y en la sífilis,
en el sudor comprado en bolsa negra,
en los fragmentos de cadenas
adheridos todavía a la piel;
sin conocernos nos reconoceremos
en los ojos cargados de sueños
y hasta en los insultos como piedras
que nos escupen cada día
los cuadrumanos de la tinta y el papel.
¿Qué ha de importar entonces
(¡qué ha de importar ahora!)
¡ay! mi pequeño nombre
de trece letras blancas?
¿Ni el mandinga, bantú,
yoruba, dahomeyano
nombre del triste abuelo ahogado
en tinta de notario?
¿Qué importa, amigos puros?
¡Oh sí, puros amigos,
venid a ver mi nombre!
Mi nombre interminable,
hecho de interminables nombres;
el nombre mío, ajeno,
libre y mío, ajeno y vuestro,
ajeno y libre como el aire.

Elegía cubana

CUBA, isla de América
Central, la mayor de las
Antillas, situada a la
entrada del golfo de
México . . .
Larousse Ilustrado

Cuba, palmar vendido,
sueño descuartizado,
duro mapa de azúcar y de olvido . . .

¿Dónde, fino venado,
de bosque en bosque y bosque perseguido,
bosque hallarás en que lamer la sangre
de tu abierto costado?
Al abismo colérico
de tu incansable pecho acantilado,
me asomo y siento el lúgubre
latir del agua insomne;
siento cada latido

Having never met, we will know each other by the
    hunger,
by the tuberculosis and the syphilis,
by the sweat bought in a black market,
by the fragments of chain
still clinging to the skin;
Having never met we will know each other
by the dream-full eyes
and even by the rock-hard insults
the quadrumanes of ink and paper
spit at us each day.
What can it matter, then.
(What does it matter now!)
ah, my little name
of thirteen letters?
Or the Mandingo, Bantu,
Yoruba, Dahoman name
of the sad grandfather drowned
in notary's ink.
Good friends, what does it matter?
Oh, yes, good friends
come look at my name!
My name without end,
made up of endless names;
My name, foreign,
free and mine, foreign and yours,
foreign and free as the air.

Cuban Elegy

*CUBA—an island of
Central America, the
largest of the Antilles,
situated at the entrance
to the Gulf of
Mexico . . .*
Illustrated Larousse

Cuba: sold-out palm grove,
drawn and quartered dream,
tough map of sugar and neglect . . .

Where, fine stag,
from forest to forest to forest pursued,
will you find the forest to stop and lick the blood
of your gaping flank?
Before the choleric chasm
of your tireless, shipwrecked breast
I stand and feel the somber
thrust of sleepless waters.
I feel each throb

como de un mar en diástole,
como de un mar en sístole,
como de un mar concéntrico,
de un mar como en sí mismo derramado.
Lo saben ya, lo han visto
las mulatas con hombros de caoba,
las guitarras con vientres de mulata;
lo repiten, lo han visto
las noches en el puerto,
donde bajo un gran cielo de hojalata
flota un velero muerto.
Lo saben el tambor y el cocodrilo,
los choferes, el Vista
de la Aduana, el turista
de asombro militante;
lo aprendió la botella
en cuyo fondo se ahoga una estrella;
lo aprendieron, lo han visto
la calle con un niño de cien años,
el ron, el bar, la rosa, el marinero
y la mujer que pasa de repente,
en el pecho clavado
un puñal de aguardiente.

Cuba, tu caña miro
gemir, crecer ansiosa,
larga, larga, como un largo suspiro.
Medio a medio del aire
el humo amargo de tu incendio aspiro;
allí su cuerno erigen,
deshaciéndose en mínimos relámpagos
pequeños diablos que convoca y cita
la Ambición con su trompa innumerable.
Allí su negra pólvora vistiendo
el joven de cobarde dinamita,
que asesina sonriendo,
y el cacique tonante, breve Júpiter,
mandarín bien mandado,
que estalla de improviso, sube, sube
y cuando más destella,
maromero en la punta de una nube,
¡ay! también de improviso baja, baja
y en la roca se estrella,
cadáver sin discurso ni mortaja.

as from expanding sea,
as from contracting sea,
as from concentric sea,
a sea which seems to crash upon itself.
They know it now, they've seen it:
black women with shoulders like mahogany,
guitars with bellies like black women.
They've seen it, they repeat it:
nights in the harbor
with a great tin sky above
a sailboat floating dead.
The drum and the crocodile know it,
like the drivers, the customs
man, and the tourist
with a militant surprise.
The bottle, in whose depth a star
is drowned, has learned it too.
They've seen it, they've learned it well:
the street with a centenary child,
the rum, the bar, the rose, the sailor,
and that woman who passes suddenly
with a dagger of cane-liquor
piercing her breast.

Oh, Cuba, I see your cane moan
and grow . . .
anxious and long, long as a heavy sigh.
In the air
I breathe the acrid smoke of its burning.
There, the little demons which Ambition calls
together with her infinite trumpet
raise their horns, then quickly disappear
in myriad flashes of light.
There, cloaked in the black powder
of cowardly dynamite, is the youth
who murders with a smile.
There is the blustering *cacique* (brief Jupiter,
obsequious mandarin)
who suddenly explodes and rises . . . rises . . . rises
'til sparkling brightly at his peak,
an acrobat on the tip of a cloud,
he just as suddenly falls . . . falls . . . falls
to smash upon a rock:
a corpse without a discourse or a shroud.

Allí el tragón avaro,
uña y pezuña a fondo en la carroña,
y el general de charretera y moña
que al Olimpo trepó sin un disparo,
y el doctor de musgosa calavera,
siempre de espaldas a la primavera . . .

Afuera está el vecino.
Tiene el teléfono y el submarino.
Tiene una flota bárbara, una flota
bárbara . . . Tiene una montaña de oro
y un mirador y un coro
de águilas y una nube de soldados
ciegos, sordos, armados
por el miedo y el odio. (Sus banderas
empastadas en sangre, un fisiológico
hedor esparcen que demora el vuelo
de las moscas.) Afuera está el vecino,
rodeado de fieras
nocturnas, enviando embajadores,
carne de buey en latas, pugilistas,
convoyes, balas, tuecas, armadores,
efebos onanistas,
ruedas para centrales, chimeneas
con humo ya, zapatos de piel dura,
chicle, tabaco rubio, gasolina,
ciclones, cambios de temperatura,
y también desde luego,
tropas de infantería de marina,
porque es útil (a veces) hacer fuego . . .
¿Qué más, qué más? El campo roto y ciego
vomitando sus sombras al camino
bajo la fusta de los mayorales,
y la ciudad caída, sin destino,
de *smoking* en el *club,* o sumergida
lenta, viscosa, en fiebres y hospitales,
donde mueren soñando con la vida
gentes ya de proyectos animales . . .

¿Y nada más?—preguntan
gargantas y gargantas que se juntan.
Ahí está Juan Descalzo. Todavía
su noche espera el día.

And there the avaricious pig I see,
who wades in carnage to his knees;
and the cardboard general, his medals bright,
who scaled Olympus without a fight;
and the doctor with a mossy skull,
who thinks the joys of spring are dull . . .

Right next door our neighbor is seen,
who has the phone and the submarine.
He has a barbarous fleet, a barbarous
fleet. He has a mountain of gold,
the penthouse, and a chorus bold
of eagles: soldiers by the score
who, blind and deaf, are led to war
by hate and fear.
(Their banners,
plastered with blood, spread a physiological
stench which stops the very flies
dead in their tracks.)
Yes, the neighbor lives just off our coast,
surrounded by nocturnal ghosts.
He sends: ambassadors who plan,
pugilists, corned beef in cans,
bullets, builders of ships, screws,
ephebic onanists, convoys too,
chimneys full of smoke, gears for the machine,
the finest light tobacco, high-test gasoline,
gum for chewing, shoes of leather,
great cyclones, changes in weather,
and troops of fierce Marines, on top of all the rest:
he finds, from time to time, the bayonet speaks best.
What else? What else? Nothing but
a torn and blinded countryside, vomiting
its shadows on the road, beneath the lash
of a field boss; the fallen city
without a future; *el esmoquín* and *el club* . . .
nothing but slow, submerged, viscous peoples who die
like animals, in hospitals and delirium,
dreaming of life.

"And nothing else?," cry voices
and voices together.
Well, there's John Barefoot: his long night
waits for dawn.

Ahí está Juan Montuno,
en la bandurria el vegetal suspiro,
múltiple el canto y uno.
Está Juan Negro, hermano
de Juan Blanco, los dos la misma mano.
Está, quiero decir, Juan Pueblo, sangre
nuestra diseminada y numerosa:
estoy yo con mi canto,
estás tú con tu rosa,
y tú con tu sonrisa
y tú con tu mirada
y hasta tú con tu llanto
de punta—cada lágrima una espada.
Habla Juan Pueblo, dice:
—Alto Martí, tu azul estrella enciende.
Tu lengua principal corte la bruma
El fuego sacro en la montaña prende.
Habla Juan Pueblo, dice:
—Maceo de metal, machete amigo,
rayo, campana, espejo,
herido vas, tu rojo rastro sigo.
Otra vez Peralejo
bien pudiera marcar con dura llama
no la piel del león domado y viejo,
sino el ala del pájaro sangriento
que desde el alto Norte desparrama
muerte, gusano y muerte, cruz y muerte,
lágrima y muerte, muerte y sepultura,
muerte y microbio, muerte y bayoneta,
muerte y estribo, muerte y herradura,
muerte de arma secreta,
muerte del muerte herido solitario,
muerte del joven de verde corona,
muerte del inocente campanario;
muerte previa, prevista,
ensayada en Las Vegas,
con aviones a chorro y bombas ciegas.
Habla Juan Pueblo, dice:
—A mitad del camino,
¡ay! sólo ayer la marcha se detuvo;
siniestro golpe a derribarnos vino,
golpe siniestro el ímpetu contuvo.
Mas el hijo, que apenas
supo del padre el nombre al mármol hecho,

There's John Backlands: a verdant sigh
from his guitar,
and a song that's diverse and one.
There's John Black, brother
to John White: side by side they walk.
I'm saying, there's John People:
our own multitudinous blood;
and I with my poem,
and you with your rose,
and you with your smile,
and you with your gaze,
and you with your sharp
lament—a sword in every tear.
John People speaks; he cries,
"Great Martí, your blue star blazes yet.
Your clear voice divides the mist.
In the mountain your sacred fire glows."
John People speaks; he cries,
"Maceo of steel, friendly cane-knife,
lightning flash, bell, mirror—I follow
the scarlet path left by your wounds."
Oh, for another Peralejo
to brand with hot flames,
not the flesh of the old and beaten lion,
but the wing of the bloodthirsty eagle
that from the terrible North brings
death—maggots and death, a cross and death,
a tear and death, death and the grave,
death and microbes, death and the bayonet,
death and stirrup, death and horseshoe,
death by secret weapons,
death of the ambushed who die alone,
death of the young man crowned with laurels,
death of the innocent sextant:
predictable, a priori death,
rehearsed in Las Vegas
with a deluge of planes and blind bombs.
John People speaks; he cries,
"Midway on the road,
just yesterday, there came an evil blow
to halt our march, to break our spirit,
an evil blow to strike us down."
But the child—knowing little
of his father save a name on marble carved—

si heredó las cadenas,
también del padre el corazón metálico
trajo con él: le brilla
como una flor de bronce sobre el pecho.
Solar y coronado
de vengativas rosas,
de su fulgor armado,
la vieja marcha el héroe niño emprende:
en foso, almena, muro,
el hierro marca, ofende
y en la noche reparte el fuego puro . . .
Brilla Naceo en su cenit seguro.
Alto Martí su azul estrella enciende.

Elegia a Emmett Till

a Miguel Otero Silva

El Cuerpo mutilado
de Emmett Till, 14
años, de Chicago,
Illinois, fue extraído
del río Tallahatchie,
cerca de Greenwood,
el 31 de Agosto, tres días
después de haber
sido raptado de la
casa de su tío, por un
grupo de blancos
armados de fusiles . . .
THE CRISIS,
New York,
Octubre de 1955

En Norteamérica,
la Rosa de los Vientos
tiene el pétalo sur rojo de sangre.

El Mississippi pasa
¡oh viejo río hermano de los negros!
con las venas abiertas en el agua,
el Mississippi cuando pasa.
Suspira su ancho pecho
y en su guitarra bárbara,
el Mississippi cuando pasa
llora con duras lágrimas.

El Mississippi pasa
el Mississippi cuando pasa.
árboles silenciosos
de donde cuelgan gritos ya maduros,
el Mississippi cuando pasa,
y mira el Mississippi cuando pasa
cruces de fuego amenazante,
el Mississippi cuando pasa,
y hombres de miedo y alarido,
el Mississippi cuando pasa,
y la nocturna hoguera
a cuya luz caníbal
danzan los hombres blancos,
y la nocturna hoguera

inheriting his chains,
he also bears his father's metal heart:
it glows, a flower of shining bronze,
upon his breast.
Sun-like, with his brilliance
armed, and crowned
by retribution's rose,
a child-hero takes up the ancient cry:
by the trench, turret, and wall of stone,
cold iron pierces, wounds to the bone,
and clean flames rise to meet the sky . . .
Maceo gleams from his zenith sure.
The blue star of Martí burns pure.

Elegy for Emmett Till

for Miguel Otero Silva

The . . . mutilated
body of Emmett
Louis Till, fourteen
of Chicago, Illinois,
was recovered from
the Tallahatchie
River (on August
31) near Greenwood,
Mississippi, three
days after he had
been kidnapped at
gunpoint from his
uncle's home . . .
THE CRISIS, *New*
York, October 1955

In North America
the mariners' rose has its southern petal
stained with blood.

The Mississippi flows,
O ancient river, brother of the Black,
with open veins beneath its waters,
the Mississippi as it flows.
Its grand breast heaves
and from its deep guitar,
the Mississippi flows,
come sobs of bitter tears.

The Mississippi flows,
and the Mississippi as it flows
sees mute trees with
ripened moans for fruit;
the Mississippi flows,
and the Mississippi as it flows
knows crosses of burning fire,
the Mississippi as it flows,
and men of terror and screams,
the Mississippi as it flows,
and nocturnal bonfires
with white men dancing
in a cannibal light,
and nocturnal bonfires

87

con un eterno negro ardiendo,
un negro sujetándose
envuelto en humo el vientre desprendido,
los intestinos húmedos,
el perseguido sexo,
allá en el Sur alcohólico,
allá en el Sur de afrenta y látigo,
el Mississippi cuando pasa.

Ahora ¡oh Mississippi,
oh viejo río hermano de los negros!,
ahora un niño frágil,
pequeña flor de tus riberas,
no raíz todavía de tus árboles,
no tronco de tus bosques,
no piedra de tu lecho,
no caimán de tus aguas:
un niño apenas,
un niño muerto, asesinado y solo,
negro.

Un niño con su trompo,
con sus amigos, con su barrio,
con su camisa de domingo,
con su billete para el cine,
con su pupitre y su pizarra,
con su pomo de tinta,
con su guante de béisbol,
con su programa de boxeo,
con su retrato de Lincoln,
con su bandera norteamericana,
negro.

Un niño negro asesinado y solo,
que una roas de amor
arrojó al paso de una niña blanca.

¡Oh viejo Mississippi,
oh rey, oh río de profundo manto!,
detén aquí tu procesión de espumas,
tu azul carroza de tracción oceánica:
mira este cuerpo leve,
ángel adolescente que llevaba
no bien cerradas todavía

with a black man always burning:
the obedient Black,
his torn bowels wrapped in smoke,
his guts choked with fumes,
his abused sex . . .
there in the alcoholic South,
there in the South of insult and lash,
the Mississippi as it flows.

And now, O Mississippi,
O ancient river, brother of the Black,
now a fragile youth,
a flower from your banks,
not yet a root of your trees,
a trunk in your forests,
a stone in your bed,
a cayman in your waters . . .
scarcely a child,
a dead child, murdered, alone,
black.

A boy with his top,
his pals, his neighborhood,
a Sunday shirt,
a movie ticket,
his desk and his blackboard,
his bottle of ink,
his baseball glove,
a boxing program,
his picture of Lincoln,
a U.S. flag . . .
black.

Black, murdered, alone: this boy who tossed a rose of love
at a passing girl
who was white.

O ancient Mississippi,
O king, O heavy-cloaked river!
Here detain your train of ripples,
your azure, ocean-flowing coach:
see this slight body,
this adolescent angel
on whose shoulders

las cicatrices en los hombros
donde tuvo las alas;
mira este rostro de perfil ausente,
deshecho a piedra y piedra,
a plomo y piedra,
a insulto y piedra;
mira este abierto pecho,
la sangre antigua ya de duro coágulo.
Ven y en la noche iluminada
por una luna de catástrofe,
la lenta noche de los negros
con sus fosforescencias subterráneas,
ven y en la noche iluminada,
dime tú, Mississippi,
si podrás contemplar con ojos de agua ciega
y brazos de titán indiferente,
este luto, este crimen,
este mínimo muerto sin venganza,
este cadáver colosal y puro:
ven y en la noche iluminada,
tú, cargado de puños y de pájaros,
de sueños y metales,
ven y en la noche iluminada
oh viejo río hermano de los negros,
ven y en la noche iluminada,
ven y en la noche iluminada,
dime tú, Mississippi . . .

Elegía a Jacques Roumain

Jacques Roumain nació en Port-au-Prince en 1907. Treinta y siete años después moría en la misma ciudad. Dejó libros de cuentos y libros

Grave la voz tenía.
Era triste y severo.
De luna fue y de acero.
Resonaba y ardía.

Envuelto en luz venía.
A mitad del sendero
sentóse y dijo:—¡Muero!
(Aún era sueño el día.)

had not yet healed the scars
of where there once were wings.
Feel the absent contour of this brow,
smashed by stone and stone,
by lead and stone,
insult and stone.
Look upon this gaping breast
where once-warm blood is hard and caked.
Look, and in the night made bright
by a catastrophic moon,
the endless night of the Black
with its subterranean phosphorescence.
Look, and in the night made bright,
speak Mississippi: can you contemplate
with eyes of water gone blind,
with Titan arms indifferent,
this mourning, this crime,
this minimal death yet unavenged,
this cadaver colossal and pure?
Look, and in the night made bright,
you—so heavy with fists and birds
and dreams and metals—
look, and in the night made bright,
O ancient river, brother of the Black,
look, and in the night made bright,
look, and in the night made bright,
speak . . .
Mississippi!

**Elegy for Jacques
Roumain**

*Jacques Roumain was
born in Port-au-Prince
in 1907. Thirty-seven
years later he died in
that same city. He left
books of stories and*

A grave voice ever the same,
he thundered, burned like a flame.
Made of moon and metal clear,
he thundered, burned like a flame.

Bathed in shining light he came
and fell not far from here,
crying, "My end is near!"
The day was scarcely named.

de poemas; dejó libros
de botánica y libros de
etnología. Se marchó
una mañana de agosto,
a las diez . . .

Pasar su frente bruna,
volar su sombra suave,
dime, haitiano, si viste.

De acero fue y de luna.
Tenía la voz grave.
Era severo y triste.

¡Ay, bien sé, bien se sabe que estás muerto!
Rostro fundamental, seno profundo,
oh tú, dios abatido,
muerto ya como muere todo el mundo.
Muerto de piel ausente y de pulido
frontal, tu filosófico y despierto
cráneo de sueño erguido;
muerto sin ropa ni mortaja, muerto
flotando en aguas de implacable olvido,
muerto ya, muerto ya, muerto ya, muerto.

Sin embargo, recuerdo.
Recuerdo, sin embargo.
Por ejemplo, recuerdo su levita
de prócer cotidiano:
la de París
en humo gris,
en persistente gris
la de Paris
y la levita en humo azul del traje haitiano.
Recuerdo sus zapatos,
franceses todavía
y el pantalón a rayas que tenía
en una foto, en México, de cónsul.

Recuerdo
su cigarrillo demoníaco
de fuego perspicaz;
recuerdo su escritura de letras desligadas,
independientes, tímidas, duras, de pie, a la izquierda;
recuerdo
su pluma fuente corta, negra, gruesa, "Pelíkano,"
de gutapercha y oro;
recuerdo
su cinturón de hebilla con dos letras.
(¿O una sola? No sé, me falla,

books of poems; he left
books on botany and
books on ethnology. He
set out one morning in
August, at ten . . .

Have you seen his visage dark and brave,
tell me, Haitian, tell me soon,
and the delicate shadow he cast?

The same voice ever grave,
made of metal clear and moon;
he was so severe and sad . . .

How well I know, how plain it is that you are dead!
Fundamental aspect, profound breast:
a knocked-down god now dead
like everybody dies.
Dead with vanished flesh and polished
bone, your watchful, thoughtful,
dream-filled skull is raised.
Dead without adornment or a shroud, floating
dead in waters of implacable neglect . . .
dead, dead, dead, now dead.

However, I remember.
I remember, nonetheless.
For example I recall
his everyday official's coat
from Paris . . .
misty gray,
persisting gray,
from Paris . . .
and the blue-mist coat of his Haitian suit.
I remember still-French shoes
and pinstripe pants
in a photo of him as Consul
to Mexico.

I remember
the sagacious ash
of his demoniac cigarette.
I recall the unjoined letters of his script:
timid, independent, hard and standing . . . slanting left.
I recall
his fountain pen—a short, black, fat "Pelican,"
made of hard rubber and gold.
I recall
the two letters of his belt-buckle.
(Or, was it only one? I don't know; my memory's

se me va en esto un poco la memoria;
tal vez era una sola, una gran R,
pero no estoy seguro . . .)

Recuerdo
sus corbatas, sus medias, sus pañuelos,
recuerdo
su llavero, sus libros, su cartera.
(Una cartera de Ministro,
ambiciosa, de cuero.)
Recuerdo
sus poemas inéditos,
sus papeles polémicos
y sus apuntes sobre negros.
Quizás haya también todo ya muerto,
o cuando más sean cosas de museo
familiar. Yo las conservo,
por aquí están, las guardo.
Quiero decir que las recuerdo.

¿Y lo demás, lo otro,
lo que hablábamos, Jacques?
¡Ay, lo demás no cambia, eso no cambia!
Allí está, permanece
como una gran página de piedra
que todos leen, leen, leen;
como una gran página sabida y resabida,
que todos dicen de memoria,
que nadie dobla,
que nadie vuelve, arranca
de ese tremendo libro abierto haitiano,
de ese tremendo libro abierto
por esa misma página sangrienta haitiana,
por esa misma, sola, única abierta página
terrible haitiana hace trescientos años!
Sangre en las espaldas del negro inicial.
Sangre en el pulmón de Louverture.
Sangre en las manos de Leclerc
temblorosas de fiebre.
Sangre en el látigo de Rochambeau
con sus perros sedientos.
Sangre en el Pont-Rouge.
Sangre en la Citadelle.

bad, it fails me somewhat here.
Perhaps a single letter, a big R,
but I'm not sure . . .)

I recall
his ties, his socks, his handkerchiefs.
I recall
his keychain, books, and briefcase.
(The ambitious leather
briefcase of a minister.)
I remember
uncollected poems,
polemics,
and his notes on Blacks . . .
Perhaps all this has died with him
or at the most is stuff of family
museums. But I preserve it,
it is here; I keep it
and declare that I remember.

And what about the rest, the other thing,
what we would talk about, my friend?
Oh, all that's just the same, it doesn't change!
It's there, it stands,
a giant page of stone
that everybody reads, reads, reads . . .
a great page learned and learned
again, that each man knows by heart;
a page nobody skips,
turns back, or tears
from that tremendous, open Haitian book,
from that tremendous, open book:
that very bloody Haitian page,
that same unique and single, open,
terrible, Haitian page, three-hundred years ago!
Blood on the shoulders of the first Black.
Blood in the lung of l'Ouverture.
Blood on Le Clerc's trembling feverish hands.
Blood on the lash of Rochambeau,
with his thirsty dogs.
Blood at Pont-Rouge.
Blood at La Citadelle.

Sangre en la bota de los yanquis.
Sangre en el cuchillo de Trujillo.
Sangre en el mar, en el cielo, en la montaña.
Sangre en los ríos, en los árboles.
Sangre en el aire.
(Olvidaba decir que justamente, Jacques,
el personaje de este poema,
murmuraba a veces:—Haití
es una esponja empapada en sangre.)

¿Quién va a exprimir la esponja, la insaciable
esponja? Tal vez él,
con su rabia de siglos. Tal vez él,
con sus dedos de sueño. Tal vez él,
con su celeste fuerza ...
Él, Monsieur Jacques Roumain,
que hablaba en nombre
del negro Emperador, del negro Rey,
del negro Presidente
y de todos los negros que nunca fueron más que
      Jean
      Pierre
      Victor
      Candide
      Jules
      Charles
      Stephen
      Raymond
      André.

Negros descalzos frente al Champ de Mars,
o en el tibio mulato camino de Petionville,
o más arriba,
en el ya frío blanco camino de Kenskoff:
negros no fundados aún,
sombras, zombíes,
lentos fantasmas de la caña y el café,
carne febril, desgarradora,
primaria, pantanosa, vegetal.

El va a exprimir la esponja,
él va a exprimirla.

Blood on the boots of the Yankees.
Blood on the knife of Trujillo.
Blood in the sky, on the sea, on the mountain.
Blood on the river and in the trees.
Blood in the air.
(I forgot to say that Jacques himself,
the hero of this poem,
at times would murmur, "Haiti
is a blood-soaked sponge.")

Now who will come to squeeze the sponge, the very
thirsty sponge? Perhaps it will be he
with centenary rage. Perhaps it will be he
with dream-like hands. Perhaps it will be he
with holy strength.
He, Monsieur Jacques Roumain,
who spoke for the black
Emperor, the black King,
the black President,
and for all the Blacks who never came to more than
        Jean
        Pierre
        Victor
        Candide
        Jules
        Charles
        Etienne
        Raymond
        André—

barefoot Blacks on the Champs-de-Mars,
and on the brown and lukewarm way to Petionville;
or further up, on the cold, white road to Kenskoff.
Blacks not even born:
shadows and zombies,
languid ghosts of cane and coffee;
anxious, tearing, primary,
swampy, vegetable flesh.

He will come to squeeze the sponge,
he'll come to squeeze that sponge . . .

Verá entonces el sol duro antillano,
cual si estallara telúrica vena,
enrojecer el pávido océano.

Y flotar sin dogal y sin cadena
cuellos puros en suelta muchedumbre,
almas no, pero sí cuerpos en pena.

Móvil incendio de afilada lumbre,
lamerá con su lengua prometida
del fijo llano a la nublada cumbre.

¡Oh aurora de los tiempos, encendida!
¡Oh, mar, oh mar de sangre desbordado!
El pasado pasado no ha pasado.
Le nueva vida espera nueva vida.

Y bien, en eso estamos, Jacques, lejano amigo.
No porque te hayas ido,
no porque te llevaran, mejor dicho,
no porque te cerraran el camino,
se ha detenido nadie, nadie se ha detenido.

A veces hace frio, es cierto. Otras, un estampido
nos ensordece. Hay horas de aire líquido,
lacrimosas, de estertor y gemido.
En ocasiones logra, obtiene un río
desbaratar un puente con su brutal martillo . . .
Mas a cada suspiro nace un niño.
Cada día la noche pare un sol amarillo
y optimista, que fecunda el baldío.
Muele su dura cosecha el molino.
Álzase, crece la espiga del trigo.
Cúbrense de rojas banderas los himnos.
¡Mirad! ¡Llegan envueltos en polvo y harapos los primeros
    vencidos!

El día inicial inicia su gran luz de verano.
Venga mi muerto grave, suave, haitiano
y alce otra vez hecha puño tempestuoso la mano.
Cantemos nuestra fraterna canción, hermano.

And then a hard, Antillian sun
will see the bursting of telluric veins,
will watch a timid ocean turning red.

And watch pure necks without a collar or a chain
float high in daring masses,
not yet souls but flesh in pain.

A soaring flame of piercing heat
will flash in trenchant tongues
from plain to cloudy peak.

Oh, dawn of time in flames!
Oh, sea, oh sea of overflowing blood!
The past of yesterday has not gone by;
new life hopes for life renewed!

That's how we stand, Jacques, my far-off friend.
And just because you've gone,
and just because they've taken you—
I should say, blocked your path
—no one slows down, no one slows down.

At times it's cold, that's true. Sometimes a gunshot
deafens us, and there are hours of liquid,
weeping, wailing, death-filled air.
Other times a river grows to waste,
with brutal, hammer-force, a bridge.
But with every sigh a child is born.
But every day the night gives birth to yellow,
hopeful sun which fecundates the void.
The millstone chews a stubborn yield,
and stalks of wheat grow strong and tall.
Hymns are covered with flags of red,
and look—
in dust and rags the conquered enemy comes!

Initial days initiate a dazzling summer sun;
so come my grave and soft, dead Haitian one:
raise once more your fist, tempestuous and strong;
brother, let us sing our own fraternal song!

Florece plantada la vieja lanza.
Quema en las manos la esperanza.
La aurora es lenta, pero avanza.

Cantemos frente a los frescos siglos recién despiertos,
bajo la estrella madura suspendida en la nocturna
  fragancia
y a lo largo de todos los caminos abiertos
  en la distancia.

Cantemos, pues, querido,
pisando el látigo caído
del puño del amo vencido,
una canción que nadie haya cantado:
(Florece plantada la vieja lanza)
una húmeda canción tendida
(Quema en las manos la esperanza)
de tu garganta en sombras, más allá de la vida,
(La aurora es lenta, pero avanza)
a mi clarín terrestre de cobre ensangrentado!

Elegía Camagüeyana

¡Oh Camagüey, oh suave
comarca de pastores y sombreros!
No puedo hablar, pero me gritan
la noche, este misterio;
no puedo hablar, pero me obligan
el perfil de mi padre, su índice de recuerdo;
no puedo hablar, pero me llaman
su detenida voz y el sollozo del viento.

¡Oh Camagüey, oh santo
camposanto, santo, santo! Beso
tu piedra secular, tu frente ennegrecida;
piso con mis zapatos de retorno,
con mis pies de ida y vuelta,
el gran reposo de tu pecho.
Me veo partir como un jinete. Busco
en tu violada niebla matinal
una calle y la sigo
por entre el laberinto de mi infancia,
por entre las iglesias torrenciales,

Fruit is borne by the lance of old.
In our hands, hope shines like gold.
Our dawn advances, sure and bold.

Let us sing for centuries, new and strong,
as in nocturnal fragrance we behold
our star, our road, our history unfold.

Let us sing; beloved one
—trampling into the sand
a whip torn from the master's hand—
the song no one has ever sung:
(Fruit is borne by the lance of old)
a living song like a flag unfurled
(In our hands, hope shines like gold)
From your throat in shadows, beyond this world,
(Our dawn advances, sure and bold)
to my terrestrial copper trumpet stained with blood!

Elegy for Camagüey

Oh Camagüey, oh gentle
place of shepherds and sombreros!
I cannot speak but I am beckoned
by this mystery, by this night.
I cannot speak but am obliged
by father's profile and his pointing hand.
I cannot speak but I am called
by father's prudent voice, by moans upon the wind.

Oh Camagüey, oh sacred,
sacred, sacred ground! I kiss
your worldly stones and blackened face.
With footsteps of return,
with round-trip feet, I cross
your grand breast of repose.
I see myself, a rider, setting out; in your
violated morning mist I seek
a street and follow it
through childhood labyrinths,
torrential temples,

por entre los machetes campesinos,
por entre plazas, sangres, gritos
de otro tiempo.

Es un sueño.
Oh, mi pueblo.

La voz de una guitarra suspendida
suena, llora en el aire:

Clavel de la madrugada,
el de celeste arrebol,
ya quema el fuego del sol
tu gran corola pintada.
Mi bandurria desvelada,
espejo en que yo me miro,
desde el humilde retiro
de la ciudad que despierta,
al recordar a mi muerta,
se me rompe en un suspiro.

Andando voy. Encuentro
caballos soñolientos
y vendedores soñolientos
y borrachos de vuelta, soñolientos:
caigo, lloro; tropiezo
con gentes de otro tiempo,
con gentes de allá lejos,
que ruedan, se deslizan
de otro tiempo.

Es un sueño.
Oh, mi pueblo.

Si yo pudiera
confiar a una guitarra compañera
mi pena simple, cantaría:

Aquí estoy ¡oh tierra mía!
en tus calles empedradas,
donde de niño, en bandadas
con otros niños, corría.
¡Puñal de melancolía
este que me va a matar,

peasants' cane-knives,
and the plazas, bloods and screams
of other times.

Of town of mine . . .
it is a dream.

The voice of a guitar hangs
in the air; it dreams and cries:

Oh flower of morning's light,
come new to life at dawn,
now hot sun falls upon
your petals, soft and white.
My bandore of the night,
a mirror to my soul,
from its humble repose
to the town awake again
recalls my awful pain
and sheds sweet tears of gold.

I am walking. I meet
dreamy horses,
dreamy vendors,
dreamy home-bound drunks.
I fall, I cry, I stumble
on the men of yesterday;
on far-off men
who whirl and flow
from other times.

Oh town of mine . . .
it is a dream.

If I could confide
my plain lament
to a friendly guitar, I'd sing:

I know again this land so fine
and walk these streets of stone
where years ago I, hardly grown,
would while away the time.
Oh lament, oh pain of mine,
which tears my very soul,

pues si alcancé a regresar,
me siento, desde que vine,
como en la sala de un cine,
viendo mi vida pasar!

Repito nombres ya desabrigados,
a la intemperie; nombres como huesos
de antepasados prehistóricos.
(Mi prehistoria: ayer apenas,
hoy mismo todavia y mañana tal vez.)
¿Dónde está Ñico López, farmacéutico
y amigo? ¿Dónde está, por ejemplo,
Esteban Cores, empleado
municipal, redonda cara roja
con su voz suave y ronca?
¿A dónde fue mi abuela pequeñita,
caminadora pequeñita?
Pepilla pequeñita,
con su tos asfixiada y su pañuelo
de cáncer ya en el cuello,
mi abuela pequeñita?
¿Y el policía Caanmañ, con altos ojos verdes
y boca de dos dientes?
¿Y dónde está Zamora, el policía
negro, corpachón de gigante,
sonrisa de hombre bueno?
(¡Zamora, que allá viene Zamora!
Era el grito de espanto
sobre mis juegos, terror de mis esparcimientos.)
¿Y mi compadre Agustín Pueyo,
que hablaba de Aristóteles
en las tertulias de "Maceo"?
De repente me acuerdo
de Serafín Toledo,
su gran nariz, su carcajada,
sus tijeras de sastre,
lo veo.
De Tomás Vélez tengo
(de Tomás Vélez, mi maestro)
el pizarrón con logaritmos
y un colmenar oscuro de abejas matemáticas
en el Callejón de la Risa.
Apeles Pla me espera,
pintor municipal de viento y polvo,

I'm seated in this place of old
as in a theater, and I see
a tender film upon the screen
where my life story is told.

I call out names abandoned
to the elements, names like bones
of prehistoric ancestors.
(My prehistory: scarcely yesterday,
still this very day, perhaps beyond.)
Where is Ñico López, pharmacist
and friend? For example, where's
the round, red face
and soft, hoarse voice
of Esteban Cores, city clerk?
Where did my little grandmother go?
Tiny Pepilla
with her diminutive step,
her smothered cough, and cancerous
handkerchief around her neck . . .
my little grandmother.
Where is Caanmañ, the cop with sharp green eyes
and a two-teeth mouth?
What about Zamora, the black cop
with a giant's body
and a good-guy's smile?
(Zamora! Here comes Zamora!:
the cry that frightened me at play
and terrorized my pranks.)
And my companion, Augustín Pueyo
who spoke of Aristotle
at our "Maceo" get-togethers?
Suddenly I remember
the big nose, the hearty laugh
and tailor's shears
of Serafín Toledo . . .
I can see him now.
From Tomás Vélez
(Tomás Vélez, my teacher)
comes the writing board with logarithms
and that dark hive of mathematical bees
on Risa Street.
Apeles Pla is waiting:
the local painter of dust and wind,

el Enemigo Bueno,
diablo mayor, que me enseñó
la primera mujer y el primer trago.
¿Y aquel ancho periódico
donde el señor Bielsa desataba
ríos editoriales? ¿Dónde está el coche,
con su tin-tán, tin-tán,
con su tin-tán el coche
de Don Miguel Ramírez, médico
quebradizo y panal que tuvo fuerzas
para arrancarme de raíz? Encuentro
en un recodo del recuerdo,
frente a un muro de plomos alfabetos,
a Próspero Carreras, el tipógrafo
casi mongol, breve chispazo eléctrico
allá en la suave imprenta provinciana
de mi niñez. Ahí pasa
Cándido Salazar, que repartía
de barrio en barrio y sueño liberal,
repartía
con su perfil de emperador romano,
repartía
bajo un cielo de estrellas y murciélagos,
en la noche reciente repartía
rosas de tinta y sangre
cortadas por mi padre para el pueblo.
Calle del Hospital, recorro
tu antigua piel de barro mordida por el viento.
No olvidé, no he olvidado,
calle de San Ignacio,
el gran balcón aéreo
de la terrestre casa donde soñó don Sixto,
que fue abogado y mi padrino,
Búscame, calle de San Miguel, de nuevo
aquel pupitre público
lleno de cicatrices cortaplumas
y el aula pajarera, fino trueno
colmenar y la ancha voz metálica
de Luis Manuel de Varona.

Vengo de andar y aquí me quedo,
con mi pueblo.
Vengo con mis recuerdos,
vengo con mis heridas y mis versos.

the Benign Enemy
and major demon, who showed me
my first woman, my first drink.
And that ample journal
where Sr. Bielsa undammed
editorial rivers? Oh where's the car
(the rattle-rattle, rattle-rattle,
rattle-rattle car) of Don Miguel Ramírez:
a weak and broken doctor
who had the strength
to bring me into the world? I meet
in a corner of my memory,
at his wall of lead letters,
Próspero Carreras: the almost-Mongol
typesetter, a brief electric spark
there in the quiet provincial printing house
of my boyhood. And there goes
Cándido Salazar: sharing,
from neighborhood to neighborhood, the liberal dream;
sharing,
with his Roman-emperor profile;
sharing,
beneath a sky of stars and fireflies;
sharing in the newly-fallen night
roses of ink and blood
cut by my father for the people.
Hospital Street, I survey
your ancient hide of clay, now wasted by the wind.
I did not forget, I have remembered
San Ignacio Street
and the great steel balcony
of a stucco house wherein Don Sixto slept:
he was a lawyer and my patron.
San Miguel Street, give me once again
the school desk
full of penknife scars
in an aviary-classroom with its hive-like
murmur, and the broad metallic voice
of Luís Manuel de Varona.

I come from walking far, and I remain
with my people.
I come with my memories.
I come with my wounds and my verse.

Mi madre está en la ventana
de mi casa cuando llego;
ella, que fue llanto y ruego,
cuando partí una mañana.
De su cabellera cana
toma ejemplo el algodón,
y de sus ojos, que son
ojos de suave paloma,
latiendo de nuevo, toma
nueva luz mi corazón.

Vengo de andar y aquí me hundo, en esta espuma.
Vengo de andar y aquí me tiendo, en esta hierba.
Aquí vengo a jugar, en esta plaza.
Aquí vengo a cantar, bajo estas nubes,
junto a verdes guitarras temblorosas,
de muslos entreabiertos.
Gente de urgencia diaria,
voces, gargantas, uñas
de la calle, límpidas almas cotidianas,
héroes no, fondo de historia,
sabed que os hablo y sueño,
sabed que os busco en medio de la noche,
en medio de la noche,
sabed os busco en medio de la noche,
la noche, este silencio,
en medio de la noche y la esperanza.

Elegía a Jesús Menéndez

Nacido entre las cañas,
muerto luchando por
ellas, Jesús Menéndez
fue el más alto líder
de los trabajadores
cubanos del azúcar.
Cayó asesinado en la
ciudad de Manzanillo,
el 22 de enero de 1948.

I

Las cañas iban y venían
desesperadas, agitando
las manos.
Te avisaban la muerte,
la espalda rota y el disparo.
El capitán de plomo y cuero,
de diente y plomo y cuero te enseñaban;
de pezuña y mandíbula,
de ojo de selva y trópico,
sentado en su pistola el capitán.
¡Con qué voz te llamaban,

My loving mother is waiting there
at the cottage window as I come;
when I set out she was the one
to see me off with tears and prayer.
By the waves of her pure white hair
the finest flax is put to shame;
and in her eyes which are the same
as the eyes of a peaceful dove
there shines a tender mother's love
to warm my heart with its flame.

I come from walking far, and sink into these waves.
I come from walking far, and stretch out on this grass.
Here I've come to play, in this plaza.
Here I've come to sing, beneath these clouds,
and close to the verdant trembling guitars
of parted thighs.
People of daily needs,
voices, throats, nails
in the street; limpid, quotidian, unheroic
souls; bedrock of history:
know I speak and dream of you.
Know I seek you in the middle of the night,
in the middle of the night.
Know I seek you in the middle of the night . . .
the night, this silence,
in the middle of the night, and hope.

Elegy for Jesús Menéndez

Born in the canefields, Jesús Menéndez died fighting for them. The greatest leader of Cuban sugarcane workers, he was murdered in the city of Manzanillo, 22 January 1948.

I

To and fro the troubled cane-stalks blew,
warning you
with trembling hands:
the shot, a shattered bone,
your death.
They spoke to you of lead and leather,
of the fang and lead and leather captain
squatting by his gun
with a jaw-bone and a cloven hoof,
the tropical jungle-eyed captain.
Oh, how they called you,

. . . *armado*
más de valor que
de acero.
Góngora

te lo decían,
cañas
desesperadas,
agitando las manos!
Allí estaba,
la boca líquida entreabierta,
el salto próximo esculpido
bajo la piel eléctrica,
sentado en su pistola el capitán.
Allí estaba,
las narices venteando
tus venas inmediatas,
casi ya derramadas,
el ojo fijo en tu pulmón,
el odio recto hacia tu voz,
sentado en su pistola el capitán.

Cañas
desesperadas
te avisaban,
agitando las manos.

Tú andabas entre ellas. Sonreías
en tu estatura primordial y ardías.
Violento azúcar en tu voz de mando,
con su luz de relámpago nocturno
iba de yanqui en yanqui resonando.
De pronto, el golpe de la pólvora. El zarpazo
puesto en la punta de un rugido,
y el capitán de plomo y cuero
el capitán de diente y plomo y cuero,
ya en tu incansable, en tu marítima,
ya en tu profunda sangre sumergido.

II

. . . *Hubo muchos*
valores que se
destacaron.
New York Herald
Tribune
Sección Financiera

Al fin sangre solar caída,
disuelta en agrio charco sobre azúcar.
Al fin arteria rota;
sangre anunciada, en venta
una mañana de la Bolsa
de Nueva York. Sangre anunciada, en venta

. . . armed more with
daring than with steel.
Gongora

blowing to and fro,
the troubled cane-stalks
warning you
with trembling hands.
There he was:
a moist, half-opened mouth,
his next move prefigured
beneath electric skin;
the captain, squatting by his gun.
There he was:
nostrils flared
at the about-to-be-spilled blood
of your tender veins,
his eyes fixed on your lung,
an inflexible hate for your voice;
the captain, squatting by his gun.

The troubled
cane-stalks
warning you
with trembling hands.

You walked among them, smiled
in your primordial stature, and gleamed.
The violent sugar of your powerful voice
resounded from Yankee to Yankee
like a flash of nocturnal lightning.
Suddenly the shock of gunpowder, a thud
preceded by a scream:
now the lead and leather captain,
the fang and lead and leather captain,
in your tireless, in your oceanic,
in your profound
blood
is drowned.

II

There were many
shares which rose
today.
New York Herald
Tribune.
Financial Section

At last vital blood is spilt,
dissolving over sugar in a bitter pool.
At last the ruptured artery,
blood reported one morning
on the New York
Stock Exchange. Blood reported

desde esa cinta vertiginosa
que envenena y se arrastra como una
víbora interminable de piel veloz marcada
con un tatuaje de números y crímenes.

Títulos que mejoran
o bajan medio punto.

Bonos sin vencimiento que ganaron
hasta el cinco por ciento de interés en un año.

La Cuban Atlantic Company
ayer martes,
operó, por ejemplo,
a veintinueve y medio con baja de dos puntos.

La Punta Alegre Sugar Company,
cerró con alza de un octavo de punto.

El Wall Street Journal anuncia
que la Minnesota and Ontario Paper Company
ganó cuatro millones
más que el año anterior. (El New York Times
bate palmas y chilla: ¡Vamos bien!)

Dow Jones comunica por un hilo exclusivo
que la Fedders Quigan Corporation
ha retirado su propuesta para
advertir las acciones comunes.

La Cuba Railroad Company
estuvo activa y firme.

La Mullings Manufacturing Company
recibió del Ejército
un colosal pedido
para fabricar proyectiles de artillería.
En fin, cotizaciones varias:

     Cuban Company Communes:
       abre con 5 puntos,
       cierra con 5⅜.

on vertiginous tape
that crawls and poisons like
an endless viper, its swift skin tattooed
with scars of numbers and crimes.

Shares that rise
or fall a half point.

Unmatured bonds that earned
up to 5% in a single year.

The Cuban Atlantic Company
last Tuesday
operated, for example,
at 29½ with a loss of two points.

The Punta Alegre Sugar Company
closed with a gain of ⅛ point.

The Wall Street Journal reports
that the Minnesota and Ontario Paper Company
shows a gain of 4,000,000
over last year (at which the New York Times
applauds and screams, "Well done!").

Dow Jones informs by private cable
that the Fedders Quigan Corporation
has withdrawn its proposal
to consider common stock.

The Cuban Railroad Company
was active and steady.

The Mullens Manufacturing Company
received a fabulous
Army contract
for artillery shells.
Finally, miscellaneous quotations:

> Cuban Co., Common Stock:
> open at 5,
> close at 5⅜.

West Indies Company,
   abre con 69 puntos,
   cierra con 69⅝.
United Fruit Company,
   abre con 31 puntos,
   cierra con 31⅛.
Cuban American Company,
   abre con 21 puntos,
   cierra con 21¾.
Foster Welles Company,
   abre con 40 puntos,
   cierra con 41⅝.

De repente
un gran trueno cuartea el techo frágil,
un rayo cae
desde aquel bajo cielo sulfúrico
hasta el salón congestionado:

Sangre Menéndez, hoy, al cierre,
150 puntos ⅞ con tendencia al alza.

El coro allí de

comerciantes
usureros
papagayos
lynchadores
amanuenses
policías
capataces
proxenetas
recaderos
delatores
accionistas
mayorales
trúmanes
macártures
eunucos
bufones
tahures;

West Indies Company:
    open at 69,
    close at 65⅜.
United Fruit Company:
    open at 31,
    close at 31⅛.
Cuban American Company:
    open at 21,
    close at 21¾.
Foster Welles Company:
    open at 40,
    close at 41⅝.

Suddenly,
thunder rends that fragile roof;
a bolt of lightning streaks
from that low, sulphuric ceiling
to the congested hall—

Blood of Menéndez, today at closing:
150⅞ with a tendency to rise!

The chorus there of

merchants
usurers
loudmouths
lynchers
flunkies
policemen
bosses
pimps
messengers
squealers
shareholders
overseers
trumans
macarthurs
eunuchs
buffoons
gamblers;

el coro allí de gente

    seca
    sorda
    ciega
    dura;

el coro allí junto a la abierta espalda
del alto atleta vegetal, vendiendo
borbotones de angustia, progonando
coágulos cotizables, nervios, huesos de aquella
descuartizada rebeldía;
una mordida
no más en el pulmón ya perforado.
Y el capitán detrás de las medallas,
cóncavo en la librea,
el pensamiento en la propina,
la voz a ras con las espuelas:
—Please, please! Come on, ladies and gentlemen!
Oh please! Come on, come on, come on!

Finalmente, este cauteloso suspiro de angustia se
escapó de un diario de la tarde:

    "Aunque las ganacias ayer fueron impresionantes,
el volumen relativamente bajo de un millón seiscientas mil
acciones da motivo para reflexionar. A pesar de la varie-
dad de razones expresadas, parece muy probable que la
mejoría haya sido de naturaleza técnica, y puede o no
resultar de un viraje de la tendencia reciente, dependi-
endo de que los promedios logren penetrar sus máximos
anteriores . . ."

El capitán partió rumbo al cuartel
con una aguja de cuajada sangre
pinchándole los ojos.

the chorus there of withered

      deaf
      blind
      hard
      people;

that chorus near the gaping shoulder
of a tall, sylvan athlete, selling
spurts of anguish, announcing
quotable nerves, clots and bones
of a drawn and quartered rebellion:
paying off
on a bullet-riddled lung.
And the captain behind his medals,
hollowness in uniform,
his mind fixed on the bribe
and voice the sound of spurs:
"Please, please! Come on, ladies and gentlemen!
Oh, please! Come on, come on, come on!"

At last this cautious, worried sigh
escapes from the afternoon paper:

    "Though yesterday's gains were indeed impres-
sive, the relatively low volume of one million, six-hun-
dred thousand shares traded gives some cause for reflec-
tion. In spite of the various explanations offered, it seems
most probable that the improvement was technical in
nature and, depending upon the ability of the averages
to surpass their previous highs, may or may not be seen as
owing to the direction of this recent tendency . . ."

The captain set out for the barracks house,
a needle of coagulated blood
piercing his eyes.

III

. . . si no hay entre
nosotros/hombre a
quien este bárbaro
no afrente?
Lope de Vega

Mirad al Capitán del Odio,
entre un buitre y una serpiente;
amargo gemido lo busca,
metálico viento lo envuelve.
En una ráfaga de pólvora
su rostro lívido se pierde;
parte a caballo y es de noche,
pero tras él corre la Muerte.

Allá donde anda su revólver
en diálogos con su machete
y le velan cuatro fusiles
el pesado sueño que duerme,
libre prisión un alto muro
su duro asilo le concede.
¡Oh capitán, el bien guardado!
Pero tras él corre la Muerte.

Quien le cuajara en nueve lunas
el violento perfil terrestre,
si doce meses lo maldice,
también lo llora doce meses.
Un angustiado puente líquido
de rojas lágrimas le tiende:
lo pasa huyendo el capitán,
pero tras él corre la Muerte.

Quien le engendró dientes de lobo
soñándole angélica veste,
el ojo fijo arder le mira
y en lenta baba revolverse.
Baja, buscándole en el bosque
cubil seguro en que esconderle:
huye hasta el bosque el capitán
pero tras él corre la Muerte.

Un mozo de dorado bozo,
de verde tronco y hojas verdes,
derrama en el viento su voz,
llora por la sangre que tiene.
¡Ay, sangre (sollozando dice)
cómo me quemas y me dueles!

Is there a man among
us this beast does not
offend?
Lope de Vega

Behold the Captain of Hate,
flanked by a buzzard and a snake.
A bitter moan pursues him;
metallic wind enfolds him.
In a sudden powder-flash
his livid face is masked.
He leaves on horseback, it is night.
But Death rides close behind.

There where his revolver
with a cane-knife converses
and where four rifles watch
his sleep of troubled dreams,
a difficult refuge grants no more
than the freedom of prison walls.
Captain, captain, guarded so well!
But Death rides close behind.

If she who fashioned nine long moons
his violent mortal form
grieves for him twelve months,
she damns him twelve months more
and offers him a bridge of sorrow
made with blood-red tears;
the captain passes, fleeing fast.
But Death rides close behind.

She who dreamed angelica flowers
but bore in him the teeth of a wolf
contemplates with steady gaze
his passage through spittle and flame.
Deep in the forest she seeks for him
a lair secure in which to hide;
the captain flees to the forest deep.
But Death rides close behind.

A lad with golden, downy cheeks
and tender as a sapling's leaf
fills the wind with deep lament
for the blood which flows in his veins.
"Oh, blood of mine," he cries with a sob;
"how you burn and torture me!"

El capitán huye en un grito,
pero tras él corre la Muerte.

Quien de sus rosas amorosas
le regaló la de más fiebre,
teje una cruel corona oscura
y es con vergüenza como teje.
Le resplandece el corazón
en la gran noche de la frente;
huye sin verla el capitán,
pero tras él corre la Muerte.

En medio de las cañas foscas
galopa el hirsuto jinete;
va con un látigo de fósforo
y el odio cuando pasa enciende
Jesús Menéndez se sonríe,
desde su pulmón amanece:
huye de un golpe el capitán,
pero tras él corre la Muerte.

IV

*Un corazón en el pecho/
de crímenes no
manchado.*
Plácido

Jesús es negro y fino y prócer, como un bastón de
ébano, y tiene los dientes blancos y corteses, por lo que su
boca se abre siempre amanecida;

Jesús brilla a veces con ojos tristes y dulces; a veces
óyese bramar en sus ojos un agua embravedica;

Jesús dice *carro, rio, ferrocarril, cigarro,* como un
francés renuente a olvidar su lengua de niño, nunca
perdida;

pero es cubano y su padre habló con Maceo; con
Maceo, que llevaba en el hombro una estrella de oro, una
ardiente estrella encendida;

alguna vez anduve con Jesús transitando de sueño
en sueño su gran provincia llena de hombres que le ten-
dían la mocha encallecida;

120

The captain flees the youthful cry.
But Death rides close behind.

He who from the gentle roses
picked for him the fiercest one
weaves a darkened, savage crown
and looks with shame on his work.
In the dark night of his aspect
a manly heart is burning bright.
The captain flees, ignoring it.
But Death rides close behind.

Through the canefields growing thick
the wild-eyed horseman gallops;
he carries a lash of phosphorus
and hate flares hot where he passes.
Jesús Menéndez, with a smile,
rises up like the morning sun;
the captain flees the vengeful blow.
But Death rides close behind.

IV

In his breast a heart
by crimes unstained.
Plácido

    Jesús is black and polished and fine, like an ebony
staff; he has polite, white teeth, which always makes his
smile like dawn.

    Jesús gleams at times with sweet, sad eyes; and in
those eyes at times impassioned waters roar.

    Jesús says *carro, río, ferrocarril, cigarro* like a
Frenchman, reluctant to cast off the boyhood speech he's
never lost.

    But he's Cuban, and his father spoke with Maceo;
with Maceo—whose shoulder bore a star of gold, a fervent
burning star.

    Once I was with Jesús, walking from dream to
dream through his great province filled with men who
greeted him with calloused cane-knives.

su gran provincia llena de hombres que gritaban
¡Oh Jesús! como si hubieran estado esperando larga-
mente su venida;

viósele entonces hablarles sin tribuna y tan cerca
de ellos que les contaba los poros y les olía la piel agria y
repartida;

se le vió luego sentárseles a la mesa de blanco
arroz y oscura carne; a la mesa sin vino ni mantel, y presi-
dirles la comida;

Jesús nació en el centro de su Isla y alli se le
descubre desde el mar, en los días claros, cubierto de
nubes fijas;

¡subid, subidlo y contemplaréis desde su frente
con qué fragor hierve a sus pies y se renueva en ondas
interminables la vida!

V

Vuelve a buscar a aquel
que lo ha herido, / y al
punto que miro, le
conocía
Ercilla

Los grandes muertos son inmortales: no mueren
nunca. Parece que se marchan; parece que se los llevan,
que se pudren, que se deshacen. Pensamos que la última
tierra que les llena la boca va a enmudecerlos para siempre.
Pero la lengua se les hincha, les crece; la lengua se les
abre como una semilla bárbara y expulsa un árbol gigan-
tesco, un árbol duro, cargado de plumas y de nidos.
¿Quién vio caer a Jesús? Nadie lo viera, ni aun su asesino. Quedó en pie, rodeado de cañas insurrectas, de cañas
coléricas. Y ahora grita, resuena, no se detiene. Marcha
por un camino sin término, hecho de tiempo sutil, polvoriento de instantes menudos, como una arena fina. No
esperes a que Jesús te bendiga y te oiga cada año, luego
de la romería y el sermón y la salve y el incienso, porque
él no espera tanto tiempo para hablarte. Ta habla siempre
como un dios cotidiano, a quien puedes tocar la piel húmeda temblorosa de latidos, de pequeñas mariposas de
fuego aleteándole en las venas; te habla siempre como
un amigo puro que no desaparece. El desaparecido es
el otro. El vivo es el muerto, cuya persistencia mineral
es apenas una caída anticipada, un adelanto lúgubre.

His great province filled with men who cried, "Oh, Jesús!," as if they'd waited long for him to come.

He was seen then to speak not from a rostrum, but so close that he could count their pores and smell their stretched and sour skin.

He was seen then to sit with them at a table of white rice and dark meat, a table without wine or linen, to preside over their meal.

Jesús was born in the center of his island, and there he can be seen, on clear days, wrapped in still clouds.

Raise, raise him up and contemplate through him how life storms at his feet and is renewed in endless waves!

V

He seeks again the man who struck the blow,/ and when he looked he knew him instantly.
Ercilla

The greatest of the dead are immortal; they never die. It only seems that they depart, are carried off, rot, disintegrate. We think the earth that fills their mouths will silence them forever. But their tongues swell, they grow. Their tongues split like barbarous seeds and send up gigantic trees, strong trees filled with nests and birds. Who saw Jesús fall? No one could have seen him, not even his assassin. He remained standing amid insurgent canestalks, choleric canestalks. And now he shouts, echoes, is not held back. He walks down a road that has no end, a road of subtle time and dusty with moments intangible as fine sand. Do not wait for Jesús to bless and hear you once each year after the pilgrimage and the sermon and the salve and the incense, for he will not be so long in speaking. He speaks to you always, like an everyday god you can touch; his humid flesh stirring with life, little moths of fire dancing in his veins. He speaks to you always, like the dear friend who never fails. It is the other one who died. The living one is dead; his mineral persistence is merely an anticipated fall, a gloomy postponement. The living one is dead. Stained with his neighbor's

El vivo es el muerto. Rojo de sangre ajena, habla sin
voz y nadie le atiende ni le oye. El vivo es el muerto.
Anda de noche en noche y amenaza en el aire con un
púno de agua podrida. El vivo es el muerto. Con un
púno de limo y cloaca, que hiede como el estómago de
una hiena. El vivo es el muerto.¡Ah, no sabéis cuantos
recuerdos de metal le martillean a modo de pequeños
martillos y le clavan largos clavos en las sienes!

Caña Manzanillo ejército
bala yanqui azúcar
crimen Manzanillo huelga
ingenio partido cárcel
dólar Manzanillo viuda
entierro hijos padres
venganza Manzanillo zafra.

Un torbellino de voces que lo rodean y golpean, o
que de repente se quedan fijas, pegadas al vidrio celeste.
Voces de macheteros y campesinos y cortadores y ferrovi-
arios. Ásperas voces también de soldados que aprietan
un fusil en las manos y un sollozo en la garganta.

Yo bien conozco a un soldado,
compañero de Jesús,
que al pie de Jesús lloraba
y los ojos se secaba
con un pañolón azul.
Después este son cantaba:

Pasó una paloma herida,
volando cerca de mí;
roja le brillaba un ala,
que yo la vi.

Ay, mi amigo,
he andado siempre contigo:
tú ya sabes quién tiró,
Jesús, que no he sido yo.
En tu pulmón enterrado
alguien un plomo dejó,
pero no fue este soldado,
pero no fue este soldado,
Jesús,
¡por Jesús que no fui yo!

blood, he cries without a voice and no one tends or hears him. The living one is dead. He passes from night to night and threatens the air with a putrid-water fist. The living one is dead. He has a lime and sewer fist; he reeks like the stomach of a hyena. The living one is dead. Oh, how many metal memories smite him like small hammers and drive long spikes into his head!

> Cane Manzanillo army
> bullet Yankee sugar
> crime Manzanillo strike
> plantation Party prison
> dollar Manzanillo widow
> burial children parents
> revenge Manzanillo harvest.

A whirlwind of voices surrounds him, strikes him, or suddenly stops—transfixed against the crystal of the sky. Voices of those who wield machetes, of peasants, of butchers, of railroad men. Rough voices too: voices of soldiers, who hold rifles in their hands and a sob deep in their throats.

> How well I know a soldier,
> a comrade of Jesús,
> who wept for him long
> and dried his tears
> upon a shawl of blue;
> and then he sang this song:

> There passed a wounded dove
> flying close to me;
> its wing shone red above.
> How well I see.

> Ah, Jesús my friend,
> I was with you to the end.
> You know who fired the gun.
> Jesús, it wasn't me.
> A bullet in your breast
> by someone on the run.
> But this soldier's not like the rest;
> but this soldier's not like the rest,
> Jesús,
> Jesús, it wasn't me.

Pasó una paloma herida,
volando cerca de mí;
rojo le brillaba el pico,
que yo la vi.

Nunca quiera
contar si en mi cartuchera
todas las balas están:
nunca quiera, capitán.
Pues faltarán de seguro
(de seguro faltarán)
las balas que a un pecho puro,
las balas que a un pecho puro,
mi flor,
por odio a clavarse van.

Pasó una paloma herida,
volando cerca de mí;
rojo le brillaba el cuello,
que yo la vi.

¡Ay, qué triste
saber que el verdugo existe!
Pero es más triste saber
que mata para comer.
Pues que tendrá la comida
(todo puede suceder)
un gusto a sangre caída,
un gusto a sangre caída,
caramba,
y a lágrima de mujer.

Pasó una paloma herida,
volando cerca de mí;
rojo le brillaba el pecho,
que yo la vi.

Un sinsonte
perdido murió en el monte,
y vi una vez naufragar
un barco en medio del mar.
Por el sinsonte perdido
ay, otro vino a cantar,
y en vez de aquel barco hundido,

There passed a wounded dove
flying close to me;
its beak shone red above.
How well I see.

Never try to tell
from on my cartridge belt;
for every bullet's there,
every one, I swear.
But it's gone for sure
(for certain it's not there)
lead that to a heart so pure,
lead that to a heart so pure,
Jesús,
was sent by hate through the air.

There passed a wounded dove
flying close to me;
its neck shone red above.
How well I see.

Oh, the sadness and fear
to know the hangman's near.
But it's sadder yet to see
he kills in order to eat.
For he will have his bread
(since anything can be)
flavored by blood of the dead,
flavored by blood of the dead,
Jesús,
and salt from a woman's tear.

There passed a wounded dove
flying close to me;
its breast shone red above.
How well I see.

A mockingbird sweetly cried
and, lost in the mountains, died.
Once while sailing free
a ship sank deep at sea.
For the bird that was lost
another sang to me;
and for the ship that was tossed,

y en vez de aquel barco hundido,
mi bien,
otro salió a navegar.

Pasó una paloma herida,
volando cerca de mí;
iba volando, volando,
volando, que yo la vi.

VI

*Y alumbrando el camino
de la fácil conquista/
la libertad levanta su
antorcha en Nueva
York.*
Rubén Darío

Jesús trabaja y sueña. Anda por su isla, pero también se sale de ella, en un gran barco de fuego. Recorre las cañas míseras, se inclina sobre su dulce angustia, habla con el cortador desollado, lo anima y lo sostiene. De pronto, llegan telegramas, noticias, voces, signos sobre el mar de que lo han visto los obreros de Zulia cuajados en gordo aceite, contar las veces que el balancín petrolero, como un ave de amargo hierro, pica la roca hasta llegarle al corazón. De Chile se supo que Jesús visitó las sombrías oficinas del salitre, en Tarapacá y Tocopilla, allá donde el viento está hecho de ardiente cal, de polvo asesino. Dicen los *bogas* del Magdalena que cuando lo condujerón a lo largo del gran río, bajo el sol de grasa de coco, Jesús les recordó el plátano servil y el café esclavo en el valle del Cauca, y el negro dramático, acorralado al borde del Caribe, mar pirata. Desde el Puente Rojo exclama Dessalines: "Traición, traición, todavia!" Y lo presenta a Defilée, loca y trágica, que le veló la muerte haitiana llena de moscas. Hierven los *morros* y *favelas* en Río de Janeiro, porque allá anunciarón la llegada de Jesús, con otros trabajadores, en el tren de la Leopoldina. Puerto Rico le enseña sus cadenas, pero levanta el puño ennegrecido por la pólvora. Un indio de México habló sin mentarse. Dijo: "Anoche lo tuve en mi casa". A veces se demora en el Perú, de plata fina y sangrienta. O bajando hacia la punta sur de nuestro mapa, júntase a los peones en los pagos enérgicos y les acompaña la queja viril en la guitarra decorosa. ¿A dónde vuela ahora, a donde va volando, más allá del cinturón de volcanes con que América defiende su ombligo torturado por la United Fruit desde el Istmo roto hasta la linde azteca? Vuela ahora, sube por el aire oleaginoso y correoso, por el aire

and for the ship that was tossed,
Jesús,
another came to be.

There passed a wounded dove
flying close to me;
higher, higher, higher
it soared. How well I see!

VI

And lighting the way to facile conquest,/ Liberty raises her torch in New York City.
Rubén Darío

Jesús toils and dreams. He walks about his island, but also goes abroad on a grand ship of fire. He passes through canefields of misery and pauses before their tender anguish to speak with the dejected cutter; he sustains and encourages him. Suddenly, telegrams, notices, voices and signs upon the sea appear to tell that he has walked among the workers of Zulia: workers, sticky with crude oil, who showed him how the derrick—a bird of bitter iron—is picking through the rock to eat their hearts. From Chile came the word that Jesús was in the somber dens of saltpeter, Tarapacá and Tocopilla, where the wind is made of heated lime and lethal dust. The rowers of El Magdalena tell that when they took him on that great river beneath a cocoa-butter sun he pointed out the servile banana and enslaved coffee of the Cauca, and recalled the dramatic Black, chained to the shores of the Caribbean, a pirates' sea. From Pont Rouge Dessalines cries, "Treason, once again treason!," and introduces him to Defilée, wild and tragic, who watched and mourned for Haiti's fly-specked death. The shacks and favelas of Río de Janeiro go wild because news is out that Jesús is coming with other workers on the train from Leopoldina. Puerto Rico shows him her chains and raises a clenched fist, blackened by gunpowder. An Indian from Mexico spoke: "Last night he was at my house." Sometimes he stops over in the blood and fine silver of Peru. Sometimes he goes down to the southern extreme of our map to join hands with the peons of those vital districts and, like a decorous guitar, accompany their virile cry. Where is he flying now? Where is he flying? Perhaps beyond the belt of volcanoes which defend America's core, tortured from the broken isthmus to the Aztec border by United Fruit. How he

grasiento, por el aire espeso de los Estados Unidos, por
ese negro humo. Un vasto estrépito le hace volver los ojos
hacia las luces de Washington y Nueva York, donde bulle
el festín de Baltasar.

> Ahí ve que de un zarpazo Norteamérica
> alza una copa de negro metal;
> la negra copa del violento hidrógeno
> con que brinda el Tío Sam.
> Lúbrico mono de pequeño cráneo
> chilla en su mesa: ¡Por la muerte va!
> Crepuscular responde un coro múltiple:
> ¡Va por la muerte, por la muerte va!

> Aire de buitre removiendo el águila
> mira de un mar al otro mar;
> encapuchados danzan hombres fúnebres,
> baten un fúnebre timbal
> y encendiendo las tres letras fatídicas
> con que se anuncia el Ku Klux Klan,
> lanzan del Sur un alarido unánime:
> ¡Va por la muerte, por la muerte va!

> Arde la calle donde nace el dólar
> bajo un incendio colosal.
> En la retorta hierve el agua química.
> Establece la asfixia del gas.
> Alegre está Jim Crow junto a un sarcófago.
> Lo viene Lynch a saludar.
> Entre los dos se desenreda un látigo:
> ¡Va por la muerte, por la muerte va!

> Fijo en la cruz de su caballo, Walker
> abrió una risa mineral.
> Cultiva en su jardín rosas de pólvora
> y las riega con alquitrán;
> sueña con huesos ya sin epidermis,
> sangre en un chorro torrencial;
> bajo la gorra, un pensamiento bárbaro:
> ¡Va por la muerte, por la muerte va!

Jesús oye el brindis, las temibles palabras, el largo
trueno, pero no desanda sus pasos. Avanza seguido de
una canción ancha y alta como un pedazo de océano.

climbs and soars on flexible, undulant air, on oily air,
through dense air and black smoke above the U.S.A. A
great uproar draws him on toward the lights of Washington and New York where the feast of Belshazzar is raging.

There with a crash North America
raises its metal goblet of black,
the violent hydrogen goblet of black:
a toast from Uncle Sam.
And the filthy ape with a shrunken brain
shrieks from his table, "He's headed for death!"
A shadowy, multiple chorus replies,
"Death, death; he's headed for death!"

The eagle, stirring the air like a buzzard,
looks from sea to shining sea.
Below, funereal hooded forms
dance and beat a somber drum,
then light the fateful letters three
which tell of the Ku Klux Klan,
and send through the South a unanimous cry:
"Death, death; he's headed for death!"

Colossal flames consume the street
whereon the dollar is born
and seething chemicals in the retort
cause lethal gasses to form.
Next to a coffin Jim Crow smiles
and Lynch approaches to shake his hand;
the voice of their fearful lash exclaims,
"Death, death; he's headed for death!"

Secure with a cross upon his horse,
Walker lets out a mineral laugh.
Roses of gunpowder in his garden,
watered daily with kerosene.
He dreams of blood in torrents flowing
and bones stripped clean of flesh.
Beneath his hood this barbarous thought:
"Death, death; he's headed for death!"

Jesús hears the toast, the dreadful words, the long
roll of thunder—and walks on. He is carried on a broad,
deep song, like a particle of sea. Ah, but at times the

¡Ay, pero a veces la canción se quiebra en un alarido,
y sube de Martinsville un seco humo de piel cocida a
fuego lento en los fogones del diablo! Allá abajo están
las amargas tierras del Sur yanqui, donde los negros
mueren quemados, emplumados, violados, arrastrados,
desangrados, ahorcados, el cuerpo campaneando trágica-
mente en una torre de espanto. El jazz estalla en lágrimas, se muerde los gordos labios de música y espera el
día del Juicio Inicial, cuando su ritmo en síncopa ciña y
apreite como una cobra metálica el cuello del opresor.
¡Danzad despreocupados, verdugos crueles, fríos asesinos!
¡Danzad bajo la luz amarilla de vuestros látigos, bajo la
luz verde de vuestra hiel, bajo la luz roja de vuestras
hoqueras, bajo la luz azul del gas de la muerte, bajo la
luz violácea de vuestra putrefacción! ¡Danzad sobre los
cadáveres de vuestras víctimas que no escaparéis a su
regreso irascible! Todavía se oye, oímos todavía; suena,
se levanta, arde todavía el largo rugido de Martinsville.
Siete voces negras en Martinsville llaman siete veces a
Jesús por su nombre y le piden en Martinsville, le piden
en siete gritos de rabia, como siete lanzas, le piden en
Martinsville, en siete golpes de azufre, como siete piedras
volcánicas, le piden siete veces venganza. Jesús nada
dice, pero hay en sus ojos un resplandor de grávida
promesa, como el de las hoces en la siega, cuando son
heridas por el sol. Levanta su puño poderoso como un
seguro martillo y avanza seguido de duras gargantas, que
entonan en un idioma nuevo una canción ancha y alta,
como un pedazo de océano. Jesús no está en el cielo,
sino en la tierra; no demanda oraciones, sino lucha; no
quiere sacerdotes, sino compañeros; no erige iglesias, sino
sindicatos: Nadie lo podrá matar.

VII

*Apriessa cantan los
gallos/ e quieren crebar
albores.*
Poema Del Cid

¡Qué dedos tiene, cuántas
uñas saliéndole del sueño! Brilla
duro fulgor sobre la hundida zona
del aire en que quisieron destruirle
la piel, la luz, los huesos, la garganta.
¡Cómo le vemos, cómo habrá de vérsele
pasar aullando en medio de las cañas,
o bien quedar suspenso remolino,

song is fractured by a scream, and from Martinsville
there rises the dry smoke of skin cooked over the slow
flames of a diabolical fire. There below lie the bitter lands
of Yankee South where Blacks die burned, tarred and
feathered, dog-like, violated, bloodless, hanged: their
bodies toll like bells from towers of fear. Jazz breaks into
tears, chews its full music lips, and waits for the day of
Initial Judgement when the metallic cobra of its synco-
pated rhythm will catch and hold the oppressor's neck.
Dance on unconcerned, you cruel hangmen, cold assas-
sins! Dance in the yellow glow of your lash, in the green
glow of your bile, in the scarlet glow of your bonfire, in
the blue-gas glow of your death, in the purple glow of
your decay! Dance upon the corpses of victims whose
angry return you'll not escape! The long moan of Martinsville is heard today; we hear it yet: it echoes, it rises, it
burns! Seven black voices in Martinsville call the name of
Jesús seven times, and they cry in Martinsville, they cry
in seven shouts of rage like seven swords, they cry in
Martinsville with seven blasts of sulphur like seven vol-
canic rocks, they cry out seven times for their revenge.
Jesús says nothing, but the gleam of gravid promise in
his eyes is like the gleam of sunlight on a harvest scythe.
He raises his mighty fist like a sure hammer, and walks.
He is carried on a broad, deep song—sung by hearty
voices in a new tongue—like a particle of sea. Jesús is not
in Heaven, but on earth; he asks not prayers, but struggle; he wants no priests, but brothers; he founds no temples, only unions: *They cannot kill him.*

VII

Quickly calls the morn-
ing cock, as if to
shatter the dawn.
Poem of The Cid

What hands he has, how many nails
still growing as he sleeps! A bright
flame burns above the buried zone of air
in which they wanted to destroy
his flesh, his light, his bones, his voice.
How clear he shines, how clear he will be seen:
to walk among the canestalks shouting,
to hover like a cyclone in suspense,

133

o bien bajar, subir,
o bien de mano en mano
rodar como una constante moneda,
o bien arder al filo de la calle
en demorada llamarada,
o bien tirar al río de los hombres,
al mar, a los estanques de los hombres
canciones como piedras,
que van haciendo círculos de música
vengadora, de música
puesta, llevada en hombros como un himno!

Su voz aquí nos acompaña y ciñe.
Estrujamos su voz
como una flor de insomnio
y suelta un zumo amargo,
suelta un olor mojado,
un agua de palabras puntiagudas
que encuentran en el viento
el camino del grito,
que encuentran en el grito
el camino del canto,
que encuentran en el canto,
el camino del fuego,
que encuentran en el fuego
el camino del alba,
que encuentran en el alba un gallo rojo,
de pólvora, un metálico
gallo desparramando el día con sus alas.

Venid, venid y en la alta
torre estaréis, campana y campañero;
estaremos, venid,
metal y huesos juntos que saludan
el fino, el esperado amanecer
de las raíces; el tremendo hallazgo
de una súbita estrella;
metal y huesos juntos que saludan
la paloma de vuelo popular
y verde ramo en el aire sin dueño;
el carro ya de espigas
lleno recién cortadas;
la presencia esencial
del acero y la rosa:

to fall and rise,
or pass like common coin
from hand to hand;
or in the middle of our streets
hurl hot and lasting flames;
or cast into the rivers, ponds
and seas of men
his song which, like a stone,
makes rings of music
with a vengful tune, we hold
and carry on our shoulders like a hymn!

The voice that tends and embraces us,
on wakeful nights, like a flower is clasped
and from it pressed a bitter juice,
and from it pressed the humid smell
and water of his sharp-edged words
that find in the wind
a way to shout,
that find in the shout
a way to sing,
that find in the song
a way to fire,
that find in the fire
a way to dawn,
that find in dawn a scarlet cock
of dynamite and metal too,
spreading the day with its wings.

Come, come, and you will be both
bell and bell-man in that lofty spire.
Come, and we will be metal and bone
together that greet the pure
and long-awaited dawn of our beginning,
like the awesome discovery
of a sudden star.
Metal and bone together that greet
the dove of popular flight,
a bough of green in masterless air,
the cart piled high
with fresh-cut wheat,
an essential presence
of steel and the rose.

metal y huesos juntos que saludan
la procesión final, el ancho séquito
de la victoria.

Entonces llegará,
General de las Cañas, con su sable
hecho de un gran relámpago bruñido;
entonces llegará,
jinete en un caballo de agua y humo,
lenta sonrisa en el saludo lento;
entonces llegará para decir,
Jesús, para decir:
—Mirad, he aquí el azúcar ya sin lágrimas.
Para decir:
—He vuelto, no temáis.
Para decir:
—Fue largo el viaje y áspero el camino.
Creció un árbol con sangre de mi herida.
Canta desde él un pájaro a la vida.
La mañana se anuncia con un trino.

Fusilamiento

Van a fusilar
a un hombre que tiene los brazos atados.
Hay cuatro soldados
para disparar.
Son cuatro soldados
callados,
que están amarrados,
lo mismo que el hombre amarrado que van
a matar.

—¿Puedes escapar?
—¡No puedo correr!
—¡Ya van a tirar!
—¡Qué vamos a hacer!
—Quizá los rifles no estén cargados . . .
—¡Seis balas tienen de fiero plomo!
—¡Quizá no tiren esos soldados!
—¡Eres un tonto de tomo y lomo!

Metal and bone together that greet
the final procession, the broad
wave of victory.
    Then he will come:
General of the Canefields, his sabre
forged by burnished thunderbolts.
Then he will come:
astride a smoke and water steed,
with his soft smile and a slow wave.
Then he, Jesús, will come
to say,
"Behold: here is sugar without tears;"
to say,
"I have returned, do not fear;"
to say,
Long was the journey, and bitter the road.
A tree has sprung from the blood of my wound
to shelter a bird that sings of life,
and welcomes the day with its song."

Execution

They are going to execute
a man whose hands are tied.
Four soldiers
are going to shoot.
Four silent soldiers,
whose hands are tied
just like the man
they are going to kill.

"Can you escape?"
"I can't run!"
"They're going to shoot!"
"What can we do!"
"Maybe the rifles aren't loaded . . ."
"They have six bullets of fiery lead!"
"Maybe those soldiers won't shoot!"
"You're a complete idiot!"

Tiraron.
(¿Cómo fue que pudieron tirar?)
Mataron.
(¿Cómo fue que pudieron matar?)
Eran cuatro soldados
callados,
y les hizo una seña, bajando su sable,
un señor oficial;
eran cuatro soldados
atados,
lo mismo que el hombre que fueron
los cuatro a matar.

Palabras en el trópico

Trópico,
tu dura hoguera
tuesta las nubes altas
y el cielo profundo ceñido por el arco del Mediodía.
Tú secas en la piel de los árboles
la angustia del lagarto.
Tú engrasas las ruedas de los vientos
para asustar a las palmeras.
Tú atraviesas
con una gran flecha roja
el corazón de las selvas
y la carne de los ríos.

Te veo venir por los caminos ardorosos,
Trópico
con tu cesta de mangos,
tus cañas limosneras
y tus caimitos, morados como el sexo de las negras.
Te veo las manos rudas
partir bárbaramente las semillas
y halar de ellas el árbol opulento,
árbol recién nacido, pero apto
para echar a correr por entre los bosques clamorosos.

Aquí,
en medio del mar,
retozando en las aguas con mis Antillas desnudas,
yo te saludo, Trópico.

They fired.
(How could they shoot?)
They killed.
(How could they kill?)
They were four
silent soldiers,
and an officer, lowering his sword,
gave them a sign;
they were four soldiers
whose hands were tied,
just like the man
the four had gone to kill.

Words in the Tropics

Tropic,
your harsh bonfire
toasts the lofty clouds
and the deep sky girdled by the midday arc.
You dry the lizard's anguish
on the skin of trees.
You grease the wheels of the winds
to frighten the palms.
With a great crimson arrow
you pierce the heart of the jungles
and the flesh of the rivers.

Tropic,
I watch you come on the fiery roads,
with your basket of mangoes,
with your mendicant canes
and your star apples, purple as the sex of black women.
I see your rough hands
barbarously tear open seeds
and from them pull the opulent tree,
an infant tree, but able
to run among noisy forests.

Here,
in mid-sea,
in the water frolicking with my naked Antilles,
I salute you, Tropic.

Saludo deportivo,
primaveral,
que se me escapa del pulmón salado
a través de estas islas escandalosas hijas tuyas.

(Dice Jamaica
que ella está contenta de ser negra,
y Cuba ya sabe que es mulata!)

¡Ah,
qué ansia
la de aspirar el humo de tu incendio
y sentir en dos pozos amargos las axilas!
Las axilas, oh Trópico,
con sus vellos torcidos y retorcidos en tus llamas.

Puños los que me das
para rajar los cocos tal un pequeño dios colérico;
ojos los que me das
para alumbrar la sombra de mis tigres;
oído el que me das
para escuchar sobre la tierra las pezuñas lejanas.

Te debo el cuerpo oscuro,
las piernas ágiles y la cabeza crespa,
mi amor hacia las hembras elementales
y esta sangre imborrable.

Te debo los días altos,
en cuya tela azul están pegados
soles redondos y risueños;
te debo los labios húmedos,
la cola del jaguar y la saliva de las culebras;
te debo el charco donde beben las fieras sedientas;
te debo, Trópico,
este entusiasmo niño
de correr en la pista
de tu profundo cinturón lleno de rosas amarillas,
riendo sobre las montañas y las nubes,
mientras un cielo marítimo
se destroza en interminables olas de estrellas a mis pies.

A playful, springtime greeting
escaping from my salty lung
between these islands, your scandalous daughters.

(Jamaica says
she is happy being black,
and Cuba now knows she's mulatto!)

Oh,
the longing
to breath the smoke from your fire
and feel my armpits in two bitter wells!
My armpits, oh Tropic,
with their down twisted and contorted in your flames.

You give me the fists
to split coconuts like a small angry god;
you give me the eyes
to illuminate the shadow of my tigers;
you give me the ears
to hear distant claws upon the ground.

I owe you my dark body,
my agile legs and nappy hair;
my love for simple women,
this indelible blood.

I owe you the lofty days,
on whose blue cloth are pasted
round and jolly suns;
I owe you my moist lips,
the jaguar's tail and the snake's saliva;
I owe you the pond where thirsty beasts drink;
I owe you, Tropic,
this child's enthusiasm
for running on the track
of your deep waist full of yellow flowers,
laughing on the mountains, in the clouds,
while a seafaring sky
destroys itself in endless waves of stars at my feet.

Llegada

¡Aquí estamos!
La palabra nos viene húmeda de los bosques,
y un sol enérgico nos amanece entre las venas.
El puño es fuerte
y tiene el remo.

En el ojo profundo duermen palmeras exorbitantes.
El grito se nos sale como una gota de oro virgen.

Nuestro pie,
duro y ancho,
aplasta el polvo en los caminos abandonados
y estrechos para nuestras filas.
Sabemos dónde nacen las aguas,
y las amamos porque empujaron nuestras canoas bajo
      los cielos rojos.

Nuestro canto
es como un músculo bajo la piel del alma,
nuestro sencillo canto.

Traemos el humo en la manaña,
y el fuego sobre la noche,
y el cuchillo, como un duro pedazo de luna,
apto para las pieles bárbaras;
traemos los caimanes en el fango,
y el arco que dispara nuestras ansias,
y el cinturón del trópico,
y el espíritu limpio.

¡Eh, compañeros, aquí estamos!
La ciudad nos espera con sus palacios, tenues
como panales de abejas silvestres;
sus calles están secas como los ríos cuando no llueve en
      la montaña,
y sus casas nos miran con los ojos pávidos de las
      ventanas.

Los hombres antiguos nos darán leche y miel
y nos coronarán de hojas verdes.

¡Eh, compañeros, aquí estamos!
Bajo el sol

Arrival

Here we are!
The word comes to us moist from the forest,
and a vital sun rises in our veins.
Our fist is strong,
sustains the oar.

Exorbitant palms sleep in the deep eye.
The shout escapes us like a drop of pure gold.

Our foot,
tough and wide,
crushes the dust on roads abandoned
and too narrow for our ranks.
We know where the waters are born,
and love them for they pushed our canoes under the
    crimson skies.

Our song,
our simple song,
is like a muscle under the skin of the soul.

We bring the mist in the morning,
and the fire to the night,
and the knife, like a hard piece of the moon,
fit for savage skins;
we bring the alligators in the swamp,
and the bow that discharges our longings,
and the tropic's waist,
and the clear spirit.

Ah, comrades, here we are!
The city waits with its palaces, delicate
as the honeycombs of wild bees;
its streets are dry as the rivers when there's no rain in
    the mountain,
and its houses stare at us with the fearful eyes of
    windows.

The ancient men will give us milk and honey
and crown us with green leaves.

Ah, comrades, here we are!
Beneath the sun

nuestra piel sudorosa reflejará los rostros húmedos de
   los vencidos,
y en la noche, mientras los astros ardan en la punta de
   nuestras llamas,
nuestra risa madrugará sobre los ríos y los pájaros.

Pequeña letania
grotesca en la muerte
del senador McCarthy

He aquí al senador McCarthy,
muerto en su cama de muerte,
flanqueado por cuatro monos;
he aquí al senador McMono,
muerto en su cama de Carthy,
flanqueado por cuatro buitres;
he aquí al senador McBuitre,
muerto en su cama de mono,
flanqueado por cuatro yeguas;
he aquí al senador McYegua,
muerto en su cama de buitre,
flanqueado por cuatro ranas:
      McCarthy Carthy.

He aquí al senador McDogo,
muerto en su cama de aullidos,
flanqueado por cuatro gangsters;
he aquí al senador McGangster,
muerto en su cama de dogo,
flanqueado por cuatro gritos;
he aquí al senador McGrito,
muerto en su cama de gangster,
flanqueado por cuatro plomos;
he aquí al senador McPlomo,
muerto en su cama de gritos,
flanqueado por cuatro esputos:
      McCarthy Carthy.

He aquí al senador McBomba,
muerto en su cama de injurias,
flanqueado por cuatro cerdos;
he aquí al senador McCerdo,
muerto en su cama de bombas,
flanqueado por cuatro lenguas;
he aquí al senador McLengua,

our sweaty skin will reflect the moist faces of the
    vanquished,
and during the night, while stars burn on the tip of our
    flames,
our laughter will wake on rivers and birds.

**Short Grotesque Litany
on the Death of
Senator McCarthy**

Here lies Senator McCarthy
dead upon his bed of death,
watched by four monkeys;
here lies Senator McMonkey
dead upon his bed of Carthy,
watched by four buzzards;
here lies Senator McBuzzard
dead upon his bed of monkeys,
watched by four ponies;
here lies Senator McPony
dead upon his bed of buzzards,
watched by four frogs:
        Carthy McCarthy.

Here lies Senator McBulldog
dead upon his bed of howls,
watched by four gangsters;
here lies Senator McGangster
dead upon his bed of bulldogs,
watched by four screams;
here lies Senator McScream
dead upon his bed of gangsters,
watched by four bullets;
here lies Senator McBullet
dead upon his bed of screams,
watched by four sputa:
        Carthy McCarthy.

Here lies Senator McBomb
dead upon his bed of insults,
watched by four pigs;
here lies Senator McPig
dead upon his bed of bombs,
watched by four tongues;
here lies Senator McTongue

muerto en su cama de cerdo,
flanqueado por cuatro víboras;
he aquí al senador McVíbora,
muerto en su cama de lenguas,
flanqueado por cuatro buhos:
    McCarthy Carthy.

He aquí al senador McCarthy,
    McCarthy muerto,
    muerto McCarthy,
    bien muerto y muerto,
    amén.

Canción puertorriqueña

¿Cómo estás, Puerto Rico,
tú de socio asociado en sociedad?
Al pie de cocoteros y guitarras,
bajo la luna y junto al mar,
¡qué suave honor andar del brazo,
brazo con brazo, del Tío Sam!
¿En qué lengua me entiendes,
en qué lengua por fin te podré hablar,
si en yes,
si en sí,
si en bien,
si en well,
si en mal,
si en bad, si en very bad?

Juran los que te matan
que eres feliz . . . ¿Será verdad?
Arde tu frente pálida,
la anemia en tu mirada logra un brillo fatal;
masticas una jerigonza
medio española, medio slang;
de un empujón te hundieron en Corea,
sin que supieras por quién ibas a pelear,
si en yes,
si en sí,
si en bien,
si en well,
si en mal,
si en bad, si en very bad.

dead upon his bed of pigs,
watched by four vipers;
here lies Senator McViper
dead upon his bed of tongues,
watched by four owls:
       Carthy McCarthy.

Here lies Senator McCarthy,
      dead McCarthy,
      McCarthy dead,
      dead and double-dead:
      amen.

Song for Puerto Rico

Puerto Rico, member by membership
dismembered, how are you?
To the sound of guitars and coco-palms,
beneath the moon, beside the sea,
the honor is sweet to stroll arm in arm
on the arm of Uncle Sam!
In what language do you understand me?
Should I address you finally
in yes,
in *sí,*
in *bien,*
in well,
in *mal,*
in bad . . . in very bad?

They who kill you swear
you're happy. Is that true?
Your pale countenance burns and
the anemia of your gaze takes on a fatal glow
as you masticate a babble
half of Spanish, half of slang;
when they stuck you in Korea with one shove
you never knew for whom you killed:
whether for yes,
for *sí,*
for *bien,*
for well,
for *mal,*
for bad . . . for very bad!

Ay, yo bien conozco a tu enemigo,
el mismo que tenemos por acá,
socio en la sangre y el azúcar,
socio asociado en sociedad:
United States and Puerto Rico,
es decir New York City with San Juan,
Manhattan y Borinquen, soga y cuello,
apenas nada más . . .
No yes,
no sí,
no bien,
no well,
sí mal,
sí bad, sí very bad.

**Bonsal
1959**

Bonsal llegó en el viento. Este Bonsal
es el Embajador. Animal
ojiazul, peliplúmbeo, de color
rojicarne, que habla un inglés letal.
(¿Cómo se dice? ¿Bónsal? Oh, señor,
es igual.)

Sonrisas. Las sonrisas
arden como divisas.
Saludos. Los saludos
son suaves gestos mudos.
Promesas. Las promesas
anuncian largas mesas.
Y el águila imperial.
Y el dólar y el dolor.
Y el mundo occidental.
Bonsal. Este Bonsal
es el Embajador.

¿Qué quiere? Que Fidel
hable un poco con él.
Que la gente medite,
no que proteste o grite.
Que el campesino aquiete
su rifle y su machete.
Que vaya cada cual

Oh, how well I know your foe,
for we have the same thing here:
a partner in blood and sugar,
a member by membership dismembered.
United States *y* Puerto Rico,
that is to say, New York City *con* San Juan,
Manhattan and *Borinquen* . . . noose and neck;
it comes to little more than that:
not yes,
or *sí,*
or *bien,*
or well,
but *mal,*
but bad . . . but very bad!

**Bonsal
1959**

Bonsal came on the wind. Bonsal
the Ambassador. A blue-eyed,
leaden-haired animal,
with rosey-colored skin
that speaks a lethal English.
(How do you pronounce it? Bonsal?
Oh, sir, it's all the same to me.)

Smiles. The smiles
like emblems glitter.
Greetings. The greetings
gestures suave and mute.
Promises. The promises
anticipate long tables.
And the imperial eagle.
And the dollar and the pain.
And the Western World.
Bonsal. Bonsal
the Ambassador.

What does he want? He wants Fidel
to speak to him a little bit,
wants the people to meditate
and not protest or scream.
He wants the peasant to silence
his gun, still his machete.

a refrescar su ardor
con agua mineral.
Bonsal. Este Bonsal
es el Embajador.

Cuba por fin en calma. No Martí,
no Maceo. Washington es mejor.
¿El General? ¡Oh, no, la capital!
Y continuar así,
como quiere Bonsal,
que es el Embajador.
Noche. Ni un resplandor.
Sopor. Guardia Rural.
¿De acuerdo?
        —No, señor.

Alla lejos . . .

Cuando yo era muchacho
(hace, ponga el lector, cincuenta años),
había gentes grandes e ingenuas
que se asustaban con una tángana callejera
o una bulla de tragos
en un bar. Eran las que exclamaban:
—¡Dios mío, que dirán los americanos!
Para algunos
ser yanqui, en aquella época,
era como ser casi sagrado:
la enmienda Platt, la intervención
armada, los acorazados.
Entonces no era presumible
lo que es hoy pan cotidiano:
el secuestro de un coronel
gringo al modo venezolano:
o el de cuatro agentes provocadores,
como en Bolivia han hecho nuestros hermanos;
ni los definitivos barbudos de la Sierra, claro.

Hace cincuenta años,
nada menos que en la primera plana de los diarios
aparecían las últimas noticias del beisbol
venidas de Nueva York.

He wants everyone to cool off
with a mineral water drink.
Bonsal. Bonsal
the Ambassador.

Cuba calm at last. Without Marti,
or Maceo. Washington is better.
The general? Oh, no, the Capital!
And to continue just as Bonsal wants,
Bonsal who is the Ambassador.
Darkness. And not one star.
Stupor. And the Rural Guard.
Agreed?
        "No, señor."

Far Off . . .

When I was a boy
(say, reader, fifty years back)
we had grand, ingenuous people
who over a row in the street
of a hell-raising crowd in a bar
would shudder. They'd exclaim,
"Good Heavens, what would the Americans say!"
For some folks
to be a Yankee in those days
was to be something almost sacred:
the Platt Amendment, armed
intervention, battleships.
Back then, what is today quite common
was unthinkable:
the kidnapping of a gringo
colonel, like in Venezuela,
or of four *agents provocateurs,*
like our brothers did in Bolivia,
and least of all things like decisive bearded ones from
    the Sierra.

Some fifty years ago
in the first section of the newspapers, no less,
they put the latest baseball scores
direct from New York.

¡Qué bueno! El Cincinnati le ganó al Pittsburg,
y el San Luis al Detroit!
(Compre la pelota marca "Reich," que es la mejor.)

Johnson, el boxeador,
era nuestro modelo de campeón.

Para los ninos, la Castoria de Fletcher
constituía el remedio indicado
en los casos (rebeldes)
de enteritis o indigestión.

Un periódico
entre sus adelantos incluyó
una página diaria, en inglés, para los yanquis:
"A cuban-american paper
with the news of the world".

Nada como los zapatos Walk-Over
y las píldoras del Dr. Ross.

El jugo de la piña criolla
no fue más
el de ananás:
la Fruit Juice Company
dijo que era "huelsencamp".

Viajábamos por la Munson Line hasta Mobila,
por la Southern Pacific hasta Nueva Orleans,
por la Ward Line hasta Nueva York.

Había Nick Carter y Buffalo Bill.
Había el recuerdo inmediato grasiento esférico de
    Magoon,
gangster obeso y gobernador,
entre ladrones y ladrones, el Ladrón.
Había el American Club.
Había el compuesto vegetal de Lidia E. Pinkham.
Había el Miramar Garden
(con lo fácil que es *jardin* en español).
Había la Cuban Company para viajar en tren.
Había la Cuban Telephone.
Había un tremendo embajador.
Y sobre todo, ¡cuidado,
que van a venir los americanos!

Great! Cincinnati beat Pittsburgh!
St. Louis whipped Detroit!
(Buy Reich baseballs. They're the best.)

Johnson, the boxer,
was our model of a champ.

For kids, Fletcher's Castoria
was the remedy prescribed
in (rebellious) cases
of enteritis or indigestion.

One newspaper
in its table of contents listed
each day a page, in English, for the Yankees:
"A Cuban-American paper
with news of all the world."

Nothing like Walk-Over Shoes,
or the pills of Dr. Ross.

And the native pineapple juice
came no more from the plant:
the Fruit Juice Company
said it was *"huelsencamp."*

We would take the Munson Line to Mobile,
Southern Pacific to New Orleans,
and the Ward Line to New York.

We had Nick Carter and Buffalo Bill.
We had the immediate, greasy memory of fat Magoon:
obese gangster and governor,
the thief among thieves of thieves.
There was the American Club.
There was Miramar Garden
(when any fool can say *jardin* in Spanish).
To travel by train there was the Cuban Company.
There was Cuban Telephone.
There was that tremendous ambassador.
And above all there was, "Watch your step,
the Americans will intervene!"

(Otras gentes que no eran tan ingenuas
solían decir:
¡Anjá! Conque ¿van a venir,
no están aquí?)

De todos modos,
ellos sí que eran grandes,
fuertes,
honestos a más no pedir.
La nata y la flor.
Ellos eran nuestro espejo
para que las elecciones fueran rápidas y sin discusión;
para que las casas tuvieran siempre muchos pisos;
para que los presidentes cumplieran con su obligación;
para que fumáramos cigarrillos rubios;
para que mascáramos chuingón;
para que los blancos no se mezclaran con los negros;
para que usáramos pipas en forma de interrogación;
para que los funcionarios fueran enérgicos e infalibles;
para que no irrumpiera la revolución;
para que pudiéramos halar la cadena del watercloset
de un solo enérgico tirón.

Pero ocurrió
que un día nos vimos como los ninos cuando se hacen
    hombres
y se enteran de que aquel honorable tío que los sentaba
    en sus rodillas
estuvo en presidio por falsificador.
Un día supimos
lo peor.

        Cómo y por qué
mataron a Lincoln en su palco mortuorio,
        Cómo y por qué
los bandidos allá son luego senadores.
        Cómo y por qué
hay muchos policías que no están en prisión.
        Cómo y por qué
hay siempre lágrimas en la piedra de todos los
    rascacielos.
        Cómo y por qué
Tejas de un solo hachazo fue desgarrada y conducida.

Some folks, not so ingenuous
used to say,
"Hah! They'll intervene?
You mean they're not already here?"

At any rate,
they were great . . .
strong,
honest above reproach,
the cream of the crop,
and our model:
for quick elections without debate,
for buildings with many floors,
for presidents who did their duty,
for those who smoked light tobacco,
for those who used chewing gum,
for Whites who wouldn't mix with Blacks,
for those who puffed curved pipes,
for energetic and infallible functionaries,
for aborted revolution,
for a single strong tug on the chain
in the water-closet.

But it came to pass
that one day we were like children who grow up
and learn that the honorable uncle who bounced us on
    his knee
was sent up for forgery.
One day we came to know
the worst.

How and why
they murdered Lincoln in a theatre-box of death.
How and why
the bandits there become senators.
How and why
There are many cops who're not in prison.
How and why
there are tears in the stones of every skyscraper.
How and why
with one blow Texas was ripped-off and pocketed.

Cómo y por qué
no son ya de Mexico la viña ni el pomar de California.
Cómo y por qué
los infantes de marina mataron a los infantes de
Veracruz.
Cómo y por qué
vió Dessalines arriada su bandera en todos los mástiles
de Haití.
Cómo y por qué
nuestro gran general Sandino fue traicionado y asesinado.
Cómo y por qué
nos llenaron el azúcar de estiércol.
Cómo y por qué
cegaron su propio pueblo y le arrancaron la lengua.
Cómo y por qué
no es fácil que éste nos vea y divulgue nuestra simple
verdad.
Cómo y por qué.

Venimos de allá lejos, de allá lejos.
Un día supimos todo esto.
Nuestra memoria fija sus recuerdos.
Hemos crecido, simplemente.
Hemos crecido, pero no olvidamos.

Crecen altas las flores   Si yo no fuera un hombre seguro; si no fuera
un hombre que ya sabe todo lo que le espera

con Lynch en el timón, con Jim Crow en el mando
y por nocturnos mares sangrientos navegando;

si you no fuera un viejo caíman cuyo pellejo
es cada vez más duro por cada vez más viejo;

si yo no fuera un negro de universal memoria
y un blanco que conoce su pecado y su gloria;

si yo no fuera un chino libre del mandarin
mirando por los ojos de Shanghai y Pekín;

156

How and why
the vineyards and orchards of California no longer
   belong to Mexico.
      How and why
Marines killed the soldiers of Veracruz.
      How and why
Dessalines saw his flag torn from every Haitian staff.
      How and why
our great General Sandino was betrayed and murdered.
      How and why
they dirtied our sugar with manure.
      How and why
they've blinded their people and torn out its tongue.
      How and why
they're forbidden to know us and tell our simple truth.
      How and why . . .

Oh, we came from far off, from far off.
One day we learned all this.
Our mind sorts out its memories.
We've simply grown up.
We've grown
. . . but we don't forget.

The Flowers Grow High

If I were not a man secure, if I were not
a man, now wise, who knows the ghastly plot

of awful helmsman Lynch with Jim Crow in command,
whose course through nights and seas of blood is
   planned;

If I were not an ancient alligator bold
whose hide grows tougher as he grows more old;

if I were not a Black with memories of great length,
or a White who knows his weakness and his strength;

if I were not Chinese from mandarins set free,
with Shanghai and Peking now mine to keep;

si yo no fuera un indio de arrebatado cobre
que hace ya cuatrocientos años que muere pobre;

si yo no fuera un hombre soviético, de mano
multiple y conocida como mano de hermano:

si yo no fuera todo lo que ya soy, te digo
tal vez me pudiera engañar mi enemigo.

    *   *   *

Murió McCarthy, dicen. (Yo mismo dije: "Es cierto,
murió McCarthy . . ."). Pero lo cierto es que no ha
    muerto.

Vive y no esconde el bárbaro sus tenazas de hierro
y el verdugo y la silla, y el *g-man* y el encierro.

Monstruo de dos cabezas bien norteamericano,
una mitad demócrata, otra republicano;

monstruo de dos cabezas, mas ninguna con seso,
no importa que nos hable de alianza y de progreso.

Y tal vez porque habla, pues nadie en nuestra América
(india pálida y virgen, pero que no es histérica),

librado ya del férreo dogal de las Españas
va a creer a los yanquis sus tontas musarañas.

Alianza de Rockefeller con Mr. Ford: lo creo
y el progreso de entrambos no lo creo, lo veo.

Alianza de la Standard con la United . . . Pues claro,
así no es el progreso de las dos nada raro.

Alianza del Chase Bank con el World Bank. Compañero
la alianza de dos "banks" es progreso y dinero.

Pero que no me vengan con cuentos de camino,
pues yo no sólo pienso, sino además opino

en alta voz y soy antes que nada un hombre
a quien gusta llamar las cosas por su nombre.

if I were not an Indian robbed of copper ore,
for centuries dying hungry, dying poor;

if I were not a Soviet citizen whose hand
is known for helpfulness in every land;

if I were not all that I am, all I will be . . .
it's likely I'd be tricked by my enemy!

   * * *

"McCarthy died," they say; I said with them, "That's
 right."
But it's a lie; he's with us day and night.

The barbarian lives; we know his iron nails,
his hangmen, agents, torture, and his jails.

A very North American monster of two heads,
this Democrat-Republican quadruped.

A monster of two heads, and neither one with brains;
his Progress and Alliance are our chains.

So even when he speaks, America down here
(native, pale and chaste, but free from fear,

and free for evermore from Spain's oppressive ties)
will see the Yankee promises as lies.

Alliance of Rockefeller with Mr. Ford, I see:
the two make Progress; I fall to my knees.

A great Alliance of Standard and United is arranged;
the Progress of those two is nothing strange.

Alliance of Chase with World Bank, very funny;
alliances of banks means Progress for their money.

So don't recite to me excuses of great length.
These aren't ideas, but facts; I have the strength

to back them up with words and deeds. I'm not afraid
to stand and fight, to call a spade a spade.

Y pregunto y respondo y me alzo y exijo
y sé cuándo la mona cargar no quiere al hijo.

Para el yanqui no somos más que escoria barata,
tribus de compra fácil con vidrio y hojalata;

generales imbéciles sin ciencia y sin escuela,
ante el jamón colgado cada uno en duermevela;

compadres argentinos, sátrapas peruanos,
betancures, peraltas, muñoces . . . Cuadrumanos

a saltos en la selva; gente menuda y floja
que en curare mortífero sus agrias puntas moja.

Pero como tenemos bosques y cafetales,
hierro, carbón, petróleo, cobre, cañaverales,

(lo que en dólares quiere decir muchos millones)
no importa que seamos quéchuas o motilones.

Vienen pues a ayudarnos para que progresemos
y en pago de su ayuda nuestra sangre les demos.

Si en Paraguay tumultos contra Washington hay,
que vaya luego Stroessner y ayude al Paraguay.

Que quien gobierno y patria cifró en una botella,
ceda no al pueblo el mando sino a la ruda estrella

del espadón estulto cuya estulticia vende
el hogar a un etraño, y encarcela y ofende.

Que un macaco las nalgas ponga sobre el asiento
de Bolívar y ayude con terror y tormento

a que no rompa yugo si sacuda tutela
el alto guerrillero que ruge en Venezuela.

I ask and I respond, I speak and I reveal
what many times a nun's black cloth conceals.

The Yankee takes us for a filthy, worthless mass;
we're tribes he buys with toys and beads of glass.

We're untrained generals, pompous, dressed like fools
who stand before the slaughtered pig and drool.

We're Argentine *compadres,* satraps from Perú,
Muñozes, Peraltas and Betancourts too.

We're apes who bound through jungles, small, weak
   quadrupeds;
mortiferous curare drips from our arrowheads.

But since we're rich in iron, coffee, cane and rum,
in forests, copper, coal, petroleum,

(In dollars that means millions at the very least.)
who cares if we are Quechuas or beasts?

They come, enlighten us, and raise us from the mud,
to take in payment for this help our blood.

From Paraguay comes news of hate for Washington,
so Stroessner puts an end to this with guns.

And he who rules his country from the depths of cocktail glasses
hears not the peoples' voice but those of effeminate asses

whose existence is an insult, whose cruelty never fails
to sell our homes to foreigners, to put us in their jails.

So let the rump of a native fill Bolívar's fine gold
   throne
and with a militant terror, unyielding, cold as stone,

let paternalism and the horrible yoke of slavery
be smashed in Venezuela by *guerrilleros'* bravery!

Cada día en Colombia los soldados apuntan
contra los campesinos y obreros que se juntan.

Ayuda para el cobre de Chile es lo primero.
(El cobre de la "mining", no el cobre del minero).

En la montaña pura suena triste la quena.
Habla con duras sílabas de estaño cuando suena.

En Brasil, hacia el lado nordeste de su angustia,
sangre y sudor revueltos riegan la tierra mustia

donde gringos de kepis se ayudan cada día . . .
Dígalo usted, Recife. ¿No es la verdad, Bahía?

Centroamérica es una gran finca que progresa.
Va el plátano en aumento, crece el café y no cesa.

(A veces silba el látigo, se oye una bofetada,
desplómase un peón . . . En fin, eso no es nada).

Ayudador deglute su inglés y se pasea
orondo el sometido criado de vil librea

que en Puerto Rico manda, es decir obedece,
mientras la vasta frente de Albizu resplandece.

Junto al barroso Plata Buenos Aires rutila,
pero le empaña el brillo la sombra del gorila

de venenosa lengua y ojo de fija hiel,
a cuya voz se aprontan la cárcel y el cuartel.

*   *   *

Adelante, Jim Crow; no te detengas; lanza
tu grito de victoria. Un ¡hurra! por la Alianza.

Lynch, adelante, corre, busca tus fuetes. Eso,
eso es lo que nos urge . . . ¡Hurra por el Progreso!

Así de día en día (aliados progresando
bajo la voz de Washington, que es una voz de mando)

Each day in Colombia armed soldiers take pains
to kill farmers and workers who are breaking their
      chains.

So buy Chilean copper; now what could be finer?
Since it's owned by the company, not by the miner.

High in pure mountains an Indian flute sings,
but hard is the voice of the tin as it rings.

In northeast Brazil a hot anguish boils
and blood mixed with sweat irrigates a fine soil

where the gringo advisor is nothing so new . . .
Recife, Bahía: say is it not true?

And there's Central America, the best ranch around,
where banana gets better and coffee abounds.

If at times there's a whiplash or a peasant who falls,
or a rifle shot . . . why that's nothing at all.

Flashy and pompous in vile traitor's clothes,
he swaggers and chokes up what English he knows

(the leader in P.R. who merely obeys)
while the aspect of Albizu glows with bright rays.

Close by the muddy Plata, Buenos Aires lies
in a brilliance clouded by a man whose eyes

are ice, whose tongue of venom, strong but smooth,
can send you to prison for one wrong move.

                *   *   *

So forward, Jim Crow, with your voice of defiance;
don't stop til there's victory for the Alliance!

March onward Lynch; don't let your whip fall.
That's what we need: your Progress for all!

Thus day after day (allied and progressing)
Washington's voice, a voice so distressing,

hacer de nuestras tierras el naziparaíso:
ni un indio, ni un mal blanco, ni un negro, ni un mestizo;

y alcanzar la superba cumbre de la cultura
donde el genio mecánico de una gran raza pura

nos muestre la profunda técnica que proclama
en Jacksonville, Arkansas, Mississippi, Alabama

el Sur expeditivo cuyos torpes problemas
arregla con azotes, con perros y con quemas.

Sólo que en nuestra América crecen altas las flores.
Engarza el pueblo y pule sus más preciadas gemas.
De las guerrillas parten bazukas y poemas.
Con vengativa furia truenan los ruiseñores . . .

¿Puedes?

A Lumir Civrny,
en Praga

¿Puedes venderme el aire que pasa entre tus dedos
ye te golpea la cara y te despeina?
¿Tal vez podrías venderme cinco pesos de viento,
o más, quizás venderme una tormenta?
¿Acaso el aire fino
me venderías, el aire
(no todo) que recorre
en tu jardín corolas y corolas,
en tu jardín para los pájaros,
diez pesos de aire fino?

El aire gira y pasa
en un mariposa.
Nadie lo tiene, nadie.

¿Puedes venderme cielo,
el cielo azul a veces,
o gris también a veces,
una parcela de tu cielo,
el que compraste, piensas tú, con los árboles
de tu huerto, como quien compra el techo con la casa?
¿Puedes venderme un dólar
de cielo, dos kilómetros
de cielo, un trozo, el que tú puedas,
de tu cielo?

urges us on toward the culture we lack
while bad Whites, Mestizos, Indians and Blacks

are lost as we soar toward fascism's heights.
The mechanical genius of a race pure and bright

shows us techniques by which they win out
in Jacksonville, Arkansas, both North and South:

expeditious, they see to their problems, of course,
with whippings, police dogs, fires and force.

But in our America the flowers grow high
to embellish a people and sweeten the homes
of guerrillas who carry bazookas and poems . . .
with furious vengeance a nightingale cries!

Sell Me?

For Lumir Civrny,
in Prague

Can you sell me the air that moves through your fingers,
strokes your face, and smooths your hair?
Is there five *pesos* worth of wind, a cyclone's worth
of wind that you could sell me?
Perhaps there's some clean air
that I could buy,
the air (not all of it) chasing blossoms
in your garden,
in your garden for the birds . . .
a ten-*peso* measure of air.

> *The air wheels and passes*
> *in a butterfly.*
> *No one owns it, no one.*

Can you sell me sky?
The sky at times blue,
the sky at times grey,
that portion of the sky
you think you bought with the trees
of your orchard, as one buys the roof of his house.
What about a dollar's worth
of sky, two kilometers
of sky, a scrap, whatever you can spare
of your sky?

El cielo está en las nubes.
Altas las nubes pasan.
Nadie las tiene, nadie.

¿Puedes venderme lluvia, el agua
que te ha dado tus lágrimas y te moja la lengua?
¿Puedes venderme un dólar de agua
de manantial, una nube preñada,
crespa y suave como una cordera,
o bien agua llovida en la montaña,
o el agua de los charcos
abandonados a los perros,
o una legua de mar, tal vez un lago,
cien dólares de lago?

El agua cae, rueda.
El agua rueda, pasa.
Nadie la tiene, nadie.

¿Puedes venderme tierra, la profunda
noche de las raíces; dientes
de dinosaurios y la cal
dispersa de lejanos esqueletos?
¿Puedes venderme selvas ya sepultadas, aves muertas,
peces de piedra, azufre
de los volcanoes, mil millones de años
en espiral subiendo? ¿Puedes
venderme tierra, puedes
venderme tierra, puedes?

La tierra tuya es mía
todos los pies la pisan.
Nadie la tiene, nadie.

**Cualquier tiempo
pasado fue peor**

¡Qué de cosas lejanas
aún tan cerca,
pero ya definitiva-
mente muertas!

La autoridad de voz abrupta
que cobraba un diezmo al jugador
y otro diezmo a la prostituta.

The sky is in the clouds.
The clouds pass distant overhead.
No one owns them, no one.

Can you sell me rain, the water
that gives you tears and wets your tongue?
What about a dollar's worth of spring water,
or droplets from a cloud,
full and fluffy as a small lamb?
Maybe mountain rain-water,
or even water from the gutters
left to dogs.
What about a league of sea, a lake,
a hundred dollars' worth of lake?

> *Water falls and bubbles.*
> *Water bubbles and passes.*
> *No one owns it, no one.*

Can you sell me earth, the endless night
of origins, teeth
of dinosaurs, and the scattered lime
of far-off skeletons?
Can you sell me entombed jungles, dead birds,
stone fishes, or the sulphur
of volcanoes, a billion years
in rising spiral? Can you
sell me earth? Can you
sell me earth? Can you . . .

> *Your earth is mine.*
> *All feet tread it.*
> *No one owns it, no one.*

Whatever Time is Past
was Worse

How many things in the distance
are still so close
yet now definitively dead!

The authority with the abrupt voice
who collected a tithe from the gambler
and another tithe from the prostitute.

El senador (tan importante).
El representante.
El concejal.
El sargento de la Rural.
El sortijón con un diamante.

El cabaret que nunca se abrió
para la gente de color.
(Éste es un club ¿comprende?
¡Qué lástima! Si no . . .)
El gran hotel
sólo para la gente bien

La crónica de sociedad
con el retrato de la niña
cuando llegó a la pubertad.

En los bancos,
sólo empleados blancos.
(Había excepciones: alguna vez
el que barría y el ujier).

En el campo y en la ciudad,
el desalojo y el desahucio.
El juez de acuerdo con el amo.

Un club cubano de beisbol:
Primera base: Charles Little.
Segunda base: Joe Cobb.
Catcher: Samuel Benton.
Tercera base: Bobby Hog.
Short Stop: James Wintergarden.
Pitcher: William Bot.
Files: Wilson, Baker, Panther.
Sí, señor.
Y menos mal
el cargabates: Juan Guzmán.

En los diarios:
PALACIO—El Embajador
Donkey dejó al Presidente
una Nota por
el incidente
de Mr. Long

The Senator (so very important).
The Representative.
The Alderman.
The sergeant of the Rural Police.
The huge ring with a diamond.

The cabaret that never opened
to let Black people in.
(This is a club. You understand?
I am sorry! Otherwise . . .)
The great hotel
only for the well-to-do.

The society page column
with a photograph of the child
when she reached her puberty.

In all the banks,
only white employees.
(There were exceptions: occasionally
the man who swept and the usher).

In the countryside and the city,
dispossession and despair.
The judge in league with the master.

A Cuban baseball team:
First base: Charles Little.
Second base: Joe Cobb.
Catcher: Samuel Benton.
On third base: Bobby Hog.
Short Stop: James Wintergarden.
Pitcher: William Bot.
Fielders: Wilson, Baker, Panther.
Yes, sir.
And, of course,
the batboy: Juan Guzmán.

In the newspapers:
THE PALACE. Ambassador
Donkey left the President
a Note regarding
the incident between
Mr. Long

con Felo, el estibador.
(Mr. Long sigue mejor).
Los amigos de Chicho Chan
le ofrecerán un almuerzo
mañana, en La Tropical.

La vidriera,
el apuntador,
y lo peor,
sobre la acera
la enferma flor,
el triste amor
de la fletera.

En fin, de noche y de día,
¡la policía, la policía, la policía!
De noche y de día,
¡la policía, la policía, la policía!
De noche y de día
la policía.

¿No es cierto que hay muchas cosas
lejanas que aún se ven cerca,
peor que ya están definitiva-
mente muertas?

Tierra en la sierra y el llano (Son)

Al anunciarse la reforma agraria, 1959

Eres amo de mi tierra,
de los árboles y el río
    te veré.
Eres amo de mi vida,
mi vida que no es de nadie,
    sino mía,
ni siquiera de mis padres,
    sino mía.
    Te veré.

Ay, de la caña al rosal
y del rosal a la caña,
hundiendo vas tu puñal.
Te veré,
ay, como te voy a ver,
    te veré.

and Felo, the stevedore.
(Mr. Long is recovering).
The friends of Chicho Chan
will honor him with a dinner
tomorrow, at *The Tropical*.

The shop windows,
the bookie,
and worst of all
the sick flower
on the sidewalk,
the sad love
of the harlot.

In short, by night and by day,
the police, the police, the police!
By night and by day,
the police, the police, the police!
By night and by day,
the police.

Aren't there many distant
things that still seem close,
but are now definitively
dead?

**Land in the Sierra and
the Plain (Son)**

*At the announcement
of The Agrarian Reform,
1959*

You are master of my country,
of the trees and of the river
we two will meet.
Of my life you are the master,
my life that belongs to no man,
but to me
not even to my parents
but to me.
We two will meet.

From the canefield to the rosebush,
from the rosebush to the cane,
you go burying your dagger.
We two will meet,
oh, but we two will meet,
we two will meet.

171

Ayer te mandé una carta
y la escribí con mi sangre
   te veré,
para decirte que quiero,
quiero la sierra y el llano,
   Te veré.
y el río que me robaste,
el río junto a los árboles
los árboles en el viento,
el viento lleno de pájaros
   y mi vida,
mi vida que no es de nadie,
    sino mía.
   te veré,

Ay, de la caña al rosal
y del rosal a la caña,
hundiendo vas tu puñal.
   Te veré.
ay, cómo te voy a ver,
   te veré.
Vivo sin tierra en mi tierra,
sin tierrra siempre viví,
no tengo un metro de tierra
donde sentarme a morir.
   Te veré.

Con Fidel que me acompaña,
con Fidel verde y florido,
vengo a cortarte la mano,
vengo a coger lo que es mío,
   te veré,
tierra en la sierra y más tierra,
tierra en la sierra y el llano,
   te veré,
y el río junto a los árboles,
los árboles en el viento,
el viento lleno de pájaros
   y mi vida,
mi vida que no es de nadie
   sino mía.
   Te veré.

Yesterday I sent a letter
and I wrote it with my blood
we two will meet,
merely to tell you that I want,
I want the sierra and want the plain,
we two will meet,
and the river you stole from me,
the river by the forest's edge,
trees standing before the wind,
the wind full of birds
and my life,
my life which belongs to no man,
but to me.
We two will meet.

From the canefield to the rosebush,
from the rosebush to the cane,
you go burying your dagger.
We two will meet.
Oh, but we two will meet.
We two will meet.
I am landless in my country,
I've lived always without land,
I don't even have a meter
of land to lie down and die in.
We two will meet.

With Fidel as my companion,
with Fidel green and in blossom,
I am coming to slice off your hand,
I am coming to take what is mine,
we two will meet,
land in the sierra and more land,
land in the sierra and the plain,
we two will meet,
and the river by the forest,
trees standing before the wind,
the wind full of birds
and my life,
my life which belongs to no man,
but to me.
We two will meet.

I

**Guitarra en duelo
mayor**

Soldadito de Bolivia,
soldadito boliviano,
armado vas de tu rifle,
que es un rifle americano,
que es un rifle americano,
soldadito de Bolivia,
que es un rifle americano.

II

Te lo dió el señor Barrientos,
soldadito boliviano,
regalo de míster Johnson
para matar a tu hermano,
para matar a tu hermano,
soldadito de Bolivia,
para matar a tu hermano.

III

¿No sabes quién es el muerto,
soldadito boliviano?
El muerto es el che Guevara,
y era argentino y cubano,
y era argentino y cubano,
soldadito de Bolivia,
y era argentino y cubano.

IV

Él fue tu mejor amigo,
soldadito boliviano;
él fue tu amigo de a pobre
del Oriente al altiplano,
del Oriente al altiplano,
soldadito de Bolivia,
del Oriente al altiplano.

Guitar in Mourning Major

Little soldier of Bolivia,
little soldier of Bolivia,
with your rifle you go armed,
a rifle that's American,
a rifle that's American,
little soldier of Bolivia,
a rifle that's American.

II

It was given by Barrientos,
little soldier of Bolivia,
a present from Mr. Johnson
in order to kill your brother,
in order to kill your brother,
little soldier of Bolivia,
in order to kill your brother.

III

Don't you know who the corpse is,
little soldier of Bolivia?
The corpse is *el che* Guevara,
he was Argentine and Cuban,
he was Argentine and Cuban,
little soldier of Bolivia,
he was Argentine and Cuban.

IV

He was the best among your friends,
little soldier of Bolivia,
he was your friend in poverty,
from Oriente to the plateau,
from Oriente to the plateau,
little soldier of Bolivia,
from Oriente to the plateau.

V

Está mi guitarra entera,
soldadito boliviano,
de luto, pero no llora,
aunque llorar es humano,
aunque llorar es humano,
soldadito de Bolivia,
aunque llorar es humano.

VI

No llora porque la hora,
soldadito boliviano,
no es de lágrima y pañuelo,
sino de machete en mano,
sino de machete en mano,
soldadito de Bolivia,
sino de machete en mano.

VII

Con el cobre que te paga,
soldadito boliviano,
que te vendes, que te compre
es lo que piensa el tirano,
es lo que piensa el tirano,
soldadito de Bolivia,
es lo que piensa el tirano.

VIII

Despierta, que ya es de día,
soldadito boliviano,
está en pie ya todo el mundo,
porque el sol salió temprano,
porque el sol salió temprano,
soldadito de Bolivia,
porque el sol salió temprano.

V

My guitar is completely dressed,
little soldier of Bolivia,
in mourning, but is not weeping,
though it is very human to weep,
though it is very human to weep,
little soldier of Bolivia,
though it is very human to weep.

VI

It is not weeping for the hour,
little soldier of Bolivia,
is not the hour for tears and grief,
but instead for the machete,
but instead for the machete,
little soldier of Bolivia,
but instead for the machete.

VII

With the copper that he pays you,
little soldier of Bolivia,
for which you sell, and he buys,
in that alone the tyrant thinks,
in that alone the tyrant thinks,
little soldier of Bolivia,
in that alone the tyrant thinks.

VIII

Wake up, it is already day,
little soldier of Bolivia,
the whole world's now on its feet,
for the sunrise came out early,
for the sunrise came out early,
little soldier of Bolivia,
for the sunrise came out early.

IX

Coge el camino derecho,
soldadito boliviano;
no es siempre camino fácil,
no es fácil siempre ni llano,
no es fácil siempre ni llano,
soldadito de Bolivia,
no es fácil siempre ni llano.

X

Pero aprenderás seguro,
soldadito boliviano,
que a un hermano no se mata,
que no se mata a un hermano,
que no se mata a un hermano,
soldadito de Bolivia,
que no se mata a un hermano.

Lectura de domingo

He leído acostado
todo un blando domingo.
Yo en mi lecho tranquilo,
mi suave cabezal,
mi cobertor bien limpio,
tocando piedra, lodo, sangre,
garrapata, sed,
orines, asma:
indios callados que no entienden,
soldados que no entienden,
señores teorizantes que no entienden,
obreros, campesinos que no entienden.

Terminas de leer,
quedan tus ojos fijos
¿en qué sitio del viento?
El libro ardió en mis manos,
lo he puesto luego abierto,
como una brasa pura,
sobre mi pecho.

IX

Take the road that goes straight forward,
little soldier of Bolivia;
it's not always an easy road,
it's not easy always, nor smooth,
it's not easy always, nor smooth,
little soldier of Bolivia,
it's not easy always, nor smooth.

X

But then certainly you will learn,
little soldier of Bolivia,
that one does not kill a brother,
that one does not kill a brother,
that one does not kill a brother,
little soldier of Bolivia,
that one does not kill a brother.

Sunday Reading

I have spent a whole Sunday
just lying down, reading.
I in my peaceful bed,
on my fluffy pillow,
under my spotless quilt.
Feeling rock, mud, blood,
ticks, thirst,
piss and asthma:
silent Indians who do not understand,
soldiers who do not understand,
theorizing gentlemen who do not understand,
workers, peasants, who do not understand.

You finish reading,
your eyes fix
on what spot in the wind?
The book burned in my hands.
I then lay it open,
like pure coal,
on my chest.

Siento
las últimas palabras
subir desde un gran hoyo negro.

Inti, Pablito, el Chino y Aniceto.
El cinturón del cerco.
La radio del ejército
mintiendo.
Aquella luna pequeñita
colgando suspendida
a una legua de Higueras
y dos de Pucará.
Después silencio.
No hay más páginas
Esto se pone serio.
Esto se acaba pronto.
Termina.
  Va a encenderse.
Se apaga.
  Va a nacer.

Canta el sinsonte en el Turquino
  —¡Pasajeros en tránsito, cambio de avión para soñar!

—Oui, monsieur; sí, señor,
Nacido en Cuba, lejos, junto a un palmar.
Tránsito, sí, me voy.
Azúcar? Sí, señor.
Azúcar medio a medio del mar.
—¿En el mar? ¿Un mar de azúcar, pues?
—Un mar.
—¿Tabaco?
—Sí, señor.
Humo medio a medio del mar.
Y calor.
—¿Baila la rumba usted?
—No, señor; yo no la sé bailar.
—¿Inglés, no habla el inglés?
—No, monsieur, no, señor, nunca lo pude hablar.

I feel
the last words rise
from a deep black hole.

Inti, Pablito, el Chino and Aniceto.
The circle closing in.
The army radio
lying.
That tiny little moon
hanging suspended
one league from Higueras
and two from Pucara.
Then silence.
No more pages.
This is getting serious.
It will end soon.
It is ending.
  Bursting into flames.
Becoming ashes.
  Being born.

Thus Sings a Mocking-
bird in el Turquino
    Passengers in transit: change planes here to
     dream!

Oui, monsieur; sí, señor.
Born in Cuba . . . far off . . . close to the palm grove.
Yes, in transit; I'm moving on.
Sugar cane? *Sí, señor,*
a vast sea of cane.
A whole sea? You mean a sugar-sea?
A sea.
Tobacco?
Sí, señor,
a whole sea of smoke . . .
and heat.
Do you dance the rumba?
No, *señor,*
I don't know how.
English . . . don't you speak English?
No, *monsieur;* no *señor,*
I've never been able.

—¡*Pasajeros en tránsito, cambio de avión para soñar!*

Llanto después. Dolor.
Después la vida y su pasar.
Después la sangre y su fulgor.
Y aquí estoy.
Ya es el mañana hoy.

Mr. Wood, Mr. Taft,
adiós.
Mr. Magoon, adiós.
Mr. Lynch, adiós.
Mr. Crowder, adiós.
Mr. Nixon, adiós.
Mr. Night, Mr. Shadow, adiós.
Podéis marcharos, animal
muchedumbre, que nunca os vuelva a ver.
Es temprano, por eso tengo que trabajar.
Es ya tarde, por eso comienza a amanecer.
Va entre piedras el rio . . .

—¡Buenos días, Fidel!

Buenos días, bandera; buenos días, escudo.
Palma, enterrada flecha, buenos días.
Buenos días, perfil de medalla, violento barbudo
de bronce, vengativo macheta en la diestra.
Buenos días, piedra dura, fija ola de la Sierra Maestra.
Bueno días, mis manos, mi cuchara, mi sopa,
mi taller y mi casa y mi sueño;
buenos días, mi arroz, mi maíz, mis zapatos, mi ropa;
buenos días, mi campo y mi libro y mi sol y mi sangre sin
    dueño.

Buenos días, mi patría de domingo vestida.
Buenos días, señor y señora.
Buenos días, montuno en el monte naciendo a la vida.
Buenos días, muchacho en la calle cantando y ardiendo en
    la aurora.

> *Passengers in transit: change planes here to*
> *dream!*

Then lament and pain,
life and its course,
blood and flame . . .
now here I stand:
holding tomorrow in my hand.

Mr. Wood, Mr. Taft,
adiós.
Mr. Magoon, *adiós.*
Mr. Lynch, *adiós.*
Mr. Crowder, *adiós.*
Mr. Nixon, *adiós.*
Mr. Night and Mr. Shadow,
adiós.
You may leave now, piggish
rabble; may I never see you again!
It's early, I have to work.
It's late, the sun is rising.
Among the rocks a river flows . . .

> *Buenos días,* Fidel!

Buenos días, banner. *Buenos días,* shield.
Palm tree, entombed shaft, *buenos días.*
Buenos días, medallion profile, violent bearded one
of bronze, your vengeful machete raised high.
Buenos días, solid rock, resolute wave from the Sierra
    Maestra.
Buenos días, hands, spoon, soup,
shop, house, and dream.
Buenos días, rice, corn, shoes, clothing.
Buenos días, my fields, my book, my sun, and my blood
    now without a master.

My country in a Sunday suit, *buenos días.*
Ladies and gentlemen, *buenos días.*
Wilderness in the mountains come to life, *buenos días.*
Boy from the street singing and burning at dawn,
    buenos días.

Obrero en armas, buenos días.
Buenos días, fusil.
Buenos días, tractor.
Azúcar, buenos días.
Poetas, buenos días.
Desfiles, buenos días.
Consignas, buenos días.
Buenos días, altas muchachas como castas cañas.
Canciones, estandartes, buenos días.
Buenos días, oh tierra de mis venas,
apretada mazorca de puños, cascabel
de victoria . . .

El campo huele a lluvia
reciente. Una cabeza negra y una cabeza rubia
juntas van por el mismo camino
coronadas por un mismo fraterno laurel.
El aire es verde. Canta el sinsonte en el Turquino . . .

—Buenos días, Fidel.

**Vine en un barco
negrero . . .**

Vine en un barco negrero.
Me trajeron.
Caña y látigo el ingenio.
Sol de hierro.
Sudor como caramelo.
Pie en el sepo.

Aponte me habló sonriendo.
Dije:—Quiero.
¡Oh muerte! Después silencio.
Sombra luego.
¡Qué largo sueño violento!
Duro sueño.
La Yagruma
de nieve y esmeralda
bajo la luna.

Worker in arms, Right On.
Right On, rifle,
tractor,
sugar cane,
poets,
parades,
orders.
Right On, girls tall and chaste as cane stalks.
Songs and standards, Right On.
Right On, Oh land of my blood,
close formation of fists, happy bell
of victory . . .

      The countryside is fragrant with
recent rain. A black face and a white face
pass together on the same road,
crowned by the same fraternal laurel.
The very air is green. Thus sings a mockingbird in El
    Turquino . . .

      Right On, Fidel!

I Came on a Slaveship

I came on a slaveship.
They brought me.
Cane, lash, and plantation.
A sun of steel.
Sweat like a caramel.
Foot in the stocks.

Aponte, smiling, spoke to me.
I said: "Count on me!"
Oh death! Afterwards silence.
Shadows after.
A long violent sleep!
A harsh sleep.
      The Yagruma
      of snow and emerald
      beneath the moon.

O'Donnell. Su puño seco.
Cuero y cuero.
Los alguaciles y el miedo.
cuero y cuero.
De sangre y tinta mi cuerpo.
Cuero y cuero.

Pasó a caballo Maceo.
Yo en su séquito.
Largo el aullido del viento.
Alto el trueno.
Un fulgor de macheteros.
Yo con ellos.
    La Yagruma
    de nieve y esmeralda
    bajo la luna.

Tendido a Menéndez veo.
Fijo, tenso.
Borbota el pulmón abierto.
Quema el pecho.
Sus ojos ven, están viendo.
Vive el muerto.

¡Oh Cuba! Mi voz entrego.
En tí creo.
Mía la tierra que beso.
Mío el cielo.
Libre estoy, vine de lejos.
Soy un negro.
    La Yagruma
    de nieve y esmeralda
    bajo la luna.

Angela Davis

Yo no he venido aquí a decirte que eres bella.
Creo que sí, que eres bella,
mas no se trata de eso.
Se trata de que quieren que estés muerta.
Necesitan tu cráneo
para adornar la tienda del Gran Jefe,
junto a las calaveras de Jackson y Lumumba.

O'Donnell. His dry fist.
Lash and more lash.
The constables and the fear.
Lash and more lash.
My body blood and ink.
Lash and more lash.

Maceo came on horseback.
I was in his retinue.
Long the howl of the wind.
Loud the thunder.
A splendor of *macheteros*.
I was among them.
  The Yagruma
  of snow and emerald
  beneath the moon.

I see Menéndez stretched out.
Immobile, tense.
The open lung bubbles.
The chest burns.
His eyes see, are seeing.
The corpse lives.

Oh Cuba! I give you my voice.
I believe in you.
The land I kiss is mine.
Mine the sky.
I am free, I came from far off.
I am a Black man.
  The Yagruma
  of snow and emerald
  beneath the moon.

Angela Davis

I have not come to tell you you are beautiful.
I believe you are beautiful,
but that is not the issue.
The issue is they want you dead.
They need your skull
to decorate the tent of the Great Chief,
beside the skulls of Jackson and Lumumba.

Angela, y nosotros
necesitamos tu sonrisa.

Vamos a cambiarte los muros que alzó el odio,
por claros muros de aire,
y el techo de tu angustia,
por un techo de nubes y de pájaros,
y el guardián que te oculta,
por un arcángel con su espada.

¡Cómo se engañan tus verdugos! Estás hecha
de un material ardiente y áspero,
ímpetu inoxidable,
apto para permanecer por soles y por lluvias,
por vientos y por lunas
a la intemperie.
                    Perteneces
a esa clase de sueños en que el tiempo
siempre ha fundido sus estatuas
y escrito sus canciones.

Angela, no estoy frente a tu nombre
para hablarte de amor como un adolescente,
ni para desearte como un sátiro.
Ah, no se trata de eso.
Lo que yo digo es que eres fuerte y plástica
para saltar al cuello (fracturándolo)
de quienes han querido y quieren todavía, querrán
   siempre
verte arder viva atada al sur de tu país,
atada a un poste calcinado,
atada a un roble sin follaje,
atada en cruz ardiendo viva atada al Sur.

El enemigo es torpe.
Quiere callar tu voz con la voz suya,
pero todos sabemos
que es tu voz la única que resuena,
la única que se enciende
alta en la noche como una columna fulminante,
un detenido rayo,
un vertical incendio abrasador,
repetido relámpago a cuya luz resaltan

And, Angela,
we need your smile.

We are going to change the walls hate has constructed,
for the transparent walls of air,
and the roof of your anguish,
for a roof of clouds and birds,
and the guard who conceals you,
for an archangel with his sword.

How your executioners mislead themselves!
You are made of rough and glowing stuff,
a rustproof impulse,
capable of lasting through suns and rains,
through winds and moons
in the unsheltered air.
                                    You belong to
that class of dreams in which time
has always forged its statures
and written its songs.

Angela, I am not before your name
to speak to you of love like an adolescent,
or to desire you like a satyr.
That, alas, is not the issue.
I merely say that you are strong and plastic
enough to leap at (and fracture) the neck
of those who have wanted, still want, and will always
    want
to see you burned alive bound to the south of your
    country,
bound to a cindered post,
bound to a leafless oak,
bound to a burning cross alive bound to the South.

The enemy is clumsy.
He wants to silence your voice with his own,
but we all know
your voice alone resounds,
that it alone ignites
high in the night like an exploding column,
an arrested lightning flash,
a vertical consuming fire,
a recurring thunderbolt beneath whose light we glimpse

negros de ardientes uñas,
pueblos desvencijados y coléricos.

Bajo el logrado sueño donde habito
junto a los milicianos decisivos,
al agrio borde de este mar terrible pero amigo,
viendo furiosas olas romperse en la rompiente,
grito, y hago viajar mi voz sobre los hombros
del gran viento que pasa
viento mío padre nuestro Caribe.

Digo tu nombre, Angela, vocifero. Junto mis manos
no en ruegos, preces, súplicas, plegarias
para que tus carceleros te perdonen,
sino en acción de aplauso mano y mano
duro y fuerte bien fuerte
mano y mano para que sepas que soy tuyo!

blacks with fiery nails,
weakened and angry peoples.

Beneath the dream accomplished where I live
beside the decisive militia,
by the bitter edge of this terrible but friendly sea,
watching furious waves collapse on the breakers,
I yell, and make my voice travel on the shoulders
of the great passing wind
my wind our father the Caribbean.

Angela, I say your name, vociferate. I join my hands
not in pleas, entreaties, supplications, prayers
to your jailers for your pardon
but in applauding action, hand meeting hand,
hard and strong, very strong,
hand meeting hand so you will know I'm yours!

Notes and Glossary

Arranged in simple alphabetical order, these notes aim to clarify what, to the English-speaking reader, may be unfamiliar references in the text. Italics indicate lines or phrases taken directly from the text of a given poem.

Albizu Campos, Pedro
1891-1965

Apostle and martyr of Puerto Rican independence. A graduate of Harvard Law School, he was President of the Nationalist Party from the early thirties until his death. Puerto Rico having been granted autonomy from Spain in 1898, he declared the occupation by the United States an illegal transgression of the island's sovereignty, organized an army of patriots, and called for noncooperation with and armed struggle against United States imperialism. "To take our country," he vowed, "they must first take our lives." He was severely persecuted for his very effective advocacy of independence, spent many years in southern United States federal prisons and, in 1965, died of an illness contracted while in jail. A symbol of liberation to Puerto Ricans everywhere (in the United States, for example, The Young Lords Party), he is looked upon by many as the first "President of the Republic of Puerto Rico."

Aldebaran

The Eye of Hyades, a cluster in the constellation Taurus, and one of the four royal stars which, according to the ancients, watched over the heavens. One of the brightest of the stars, it is reddish in color and, coming after Pleiades, it stands for follower.

Amado, Jorge
1912-

A friend of the poet, he is one of the better known and most compelling writers of contemporary Brazil. Among his novels familiar to readers of English are *The Violent Land* (1945, 1965), *Gabriela, Clove and Cinnamon* (1962), *Shepherds of the Night* (1967), and *Doña Flor and Her Two Husbands* (1969).

Amorim, Enrique
1900-1960

A friend of Guillén, and prolific Uruguayan novelist, his works explore the gamut of social conflict that characterizes that country's rural and urban slum life. He also did a great deal of screenwriting and his career opens (*Veinte años,* 1920) and closes (*Mi patria,* 1960) with collections of poetry. His prose works include *El Paisano Aguilar* (1934), *El asesino desvelado* (1945), and *La victoria no viene sola* (1952) whose title, *Victory Comes Not by Itself,* is borrowed from Stalin.

193

Aponte, José Antonio	A free Black and a revolutionary, he organized a national insurrection among Cuban slaves in 1811: the abortive *conspiración de Aponte.* Convinced that the Spanish authorities would neither suppress the slave trade nor decree emancipation—as indeed they did not until the late 1880's—he aimed to free the slaves by force of arms and, by burning sugar and coffee plantations, to eliminate forever the economic dominance of the plantocracy. The conspiracy, however, was discovered. A period of severe repression followed, during which Aponte was captured. He was hanged, drawn and quartered on April 9, 1812. To discourage further revolt among Blacks—slave or free—his head was placed on exhibit and his hand nailed on an adjoining street.
Bahía	Brazilian state bordering on the Atlantic Ocean between Minas Gerais to the south and Maranhão, Piaui, and Pernambuco (q.v.) to the north. Mountainous agricultural region cut by several rivers, its main products are cacao, coffee, cotton, and sugar. There is some stock raising and, more recently, diamonds and oil were discovered in the region. The local music and folklore show the strong influence of Negro culture.
Betancourt, Rómulo 1908-	Venezuelan "liberal" politician. After a brief membership in the communist Party of Costa Rica (1930-31), he founded and became head of Venezuela's Acción Democrática (1941). Exiled from his country on various occasions for political reasons, he helped to bring about the fall of President Medina Angarita in 1945 and, for three years after, headed the seven-man ruling junta. In 1948, he led the Venezuelan delegation to the Ninth Pan-American Conference in Bogotá, Colombia. From the 1948 military coup through the dictatorship of Pérez Jimenez, Betancourt remained in exile. He returned after the ouster of the dictator and, in less-than-open elections concocted under the watchful eye of the United States, became President for a five-year term. In spite of his capitulation to United States economic interests and the military and other aid sent from Washington, popular dissatisfaction made it impossible for him to complete his term. However, Dr. Raul Leoni, his hand-picked successor, won the subsequent election and took office in February of 1964.

The Black Emperor	See Dessalines.
The Black King	A reference to Henri Christophe (1767-1820). Born a slave in Granada, he was subsequently freed in payment for serving bravely under Lafayette in the Battle of Savannah (1779). From the outbreak of the Haitian slave revolt of 1791, Christophe was known as a valiant soldier, and served under both L'Ouverture and Dessalines (q.v.). He seems to have been part of the conspiracy against the latter, gaining control over the northern portions of the country upon his death. He struggled constantly with Alexandre Pétion (q.v.), ruler in the south, and in 1811 had himself proclaimed Henri I, King of Haiti, giving titles of nobility to his entourage. Some nine years later, during a revolt and after having suffered two paralytic strokes, he committed suicide. Besides LaCitadelle, LaFerrière (q.v.), the Palace Sans Souci at Cap Haitien, and a body of laws, the *Code Henri,* commemorate his reign.
Bonsal, Philip 1903-	Vice-Consul in Havana in 1938, just prior to Fulgencio Batista's first rise to power (1940), he was chosen to represent the Government of the United States as its ambassador to the Revolutionary Government in 1959. He brought a history of experience representing private business and United States policy in Latin America to the post and, as Fidel Castro notes in his interview with Lee Lockwood *(Castro's Cuba, Cuba's Fidel),* "he came with the demeanor of a proconsul . . .; the reactionary press received him almost as if the Savior had come." As a result, the Premier long avoided having an interview with him.
Borinquen	From *Burenquen,* the name given to Pueto Rico by its aboriginal inhabitants. A traditional and affectionate way of referring to the island, used frequently by Puerto Ricans.
Cacique	"Chief" or "leader." The word is believed to have originated with the Araucana Indians, who inhabited what is now central and northern Chile. In contemporary Spanish it usually has pejorative connotations suggesting "tyrant" or "dictator."
Capablanca, José Raul 1888-1942	Cuban chess grandmaster, born in Havana and educated at Columbia University in New York. After learning the game from his father during his preschool years, he be-

came champion of Cuba at the age of twelve by defeating Juan Corzo. In 1909 he won the United States championship from Frank J. Marshall of the Manhattan Chess Club. More than a decade of victories in international competition established his reputation, and in 1922 he challenged and defeated 8-0 World Champion Emmanuel Lasker in Havana. He held the title until 1927 when the Russian Alexander Alekhine defeated him in Buenos Aires in a match that lasted three months. Among Capablanca's books are *My Chess Career* (1920) and *Chess Fundamentals* (1921).

Carpentier, Georges

French light-heavyweight prizefighter of the early twenties. Already considered a champion in his class in Europe, he finally became World Champion on October 12, 1920, when he met and successfully fought Barney Lebrowitz, "Battling Levinsky." It was in a match with Carpentier that, a year later, Jack Dempsey earned his title.

Carro, río, ferrocarril, cigarro

The phenomenon referred to here is Jesús Menéndez' pronunciation of the initial and double *r* like the French *rue* and *arriver,* instead of trilling them as standard Spanish would require. This type of pronunciation is not uncommon in rural, and indeed urban areas, of Cuba, Puerto Rico, and other parts of the Caribbean. People who use it are often made fun of by the "sophisticated" and more well-to-do.

Cauca

The principal tributary of the Magdalena River (q.v.) in Colombia. Its valley, also called the Cauca, is one of the most fertile and productive regions in that country.

Champ-de-Mars

As of 1913, a public park in Paris located on the Left Bank of the Seine between the river and the École Militaire. It was set aside in 1765 as an exercise and parade area for the military school. In its variants in the Caribbean and Latin America, too, it is synonymous with military parade ground.

Civrny, Lumir
1915-

Born in Prague, Dr. Civrny has worked in publishing, editing and translating, and has held various state and Party posts. In 1938 he was co-editor of an anthology of Spanish verse and in 1942 of the *Almanac of Czech Books.* The following year he edited a collection entitled *Sonnets of*

Women. During the German occupation he was a member of the then illegal Czech Communist Party and from 1946-49 was a member of its Central Committee. He was also a section head in the Ministry of Information (1946-49) and, in addition, has held posts as Deputy Minister of Information (1949-51), Deputy Minister of Education for Science & Arts (1952), and Deputy Minister of Culture (1953-57). Besides Guillén, Civrny has translated into Czech the Spanish poets Federico García Lorca, Juan Ramón Jiménez, and Rafael Alberti. He has also translated and collected German and French verse.

Crowder, Enoch Herbert 1859-1932

American soldier, lawyer, and colonial administrator-ambassador, Crowder graduated from the United States Military Academy at West Point in 1881 and received his LL.B. from the University of Missouri in 1886. During the Spanish-American War he was Judge-Advocate in the Philippines and by 1903 had achieved the rank of Colonel. He was in Cuba from 1906-09 where he served as Secretary of Justice under Magoon (q.v.) and as head of the Advisory Law Commission, revising the basic laws (civil service, electoral, treasury, etc.) of the country. After Word War I Crowder returned to Cuba as official representative of Presidents Wilson and Harding; for three or four years he helped revise election laws and procedures, imposed settlements to disputes and "advised" various politicians. As a result of his efforts a façade of United States-style "democratic procedures" was maintained without the help of Marines, and American economic interests gained a more firm hold on the island. Appointed Ambassador to Cuba in 1923, he held the post until his retirement in 1927.

Defilée

An aging and not altogether sane black woman, possibly at one time a mistress of Dessalines (q.v.), who sat by his badly mutilated body in the Place d'Armes until soldiers came to remove the assassinated emperor to an unmarked grave in the city cemetery. For a long time after she went regularly to scatter wild flowers at the place of burial. In this "Elegy for Jacques Roumain" Guillén has her mourning the *muerte haitiana* which can be rendered as "Haitian death" (that is, a death typical of or peculiar to Haiti, or as "Haiti's death." The latter was chosen here, believing the poet wished to imply that with Dessalines' death the country itself passed away in a certain sense.

Dessalines, Jean-Jacques 1758-1806	Born a slave and dying an emperor, he is one of the most controversial figures in Haiti's controversial history. With Toussaint L'Ouverture (q.v.) and Henri Christophe (q.v.), Dessalines is considered one of the country's greatest black patriots. After courageously and triumphantly leading a large number of men in the slave revolt of 1791, it was he who tore the French tricolor in three, cast the white portion into the sea, and united the red and blue portions to form the flag of independent San Dominque, renaming it Haiti. He was also instrumental in driving out the British in 1797, forming the subsequent free Black Republic, and defeating the LeClerc expedition of 1802. After Toussaint's deportation to France in 1803, be became chief of state and, a year later, was declared emperor. Two years later, he was beaten and slain by disloyal officials. "La Dessalinienne," Haiti's national anthem is named for him, as is the city Dessalines, eighteen miles southeast of Gonaïves in the Department of Artibonite in central Haiti.
Eluard, Paul 1895-1952	Pen name of Eugène Grindel. Born in St. Denis, he became one of the outstanding figures of the French surrealist movement which included fellow poets André Breton and Louis Aragón. Active in the Resistance during the Nazi occupation, he joined the Communist Party in 1942. Like Guillén's own work, his poetry blends the delicacy of the poet with the militant commitment of the man. His works include "The same day for all," "The Poem that Never Ends," and *Poésie et vérité* (1942).
el Esmoquin	from "Smoking Jacket," a formal dinner coat.
Faubus, Orval Eugene 1910-	Born in Combs, Arkansas, and educated at the State University, he rose through "the ranks" from Circuit Clerk and Recorder to Assistant Governor and finally, in 1955, to Governor, continuing in that post for twelve years. A militant advocate of the American version of apartheid, it was during his tenure as governor that, in order to insure the entrance of nine Negro students into Central High School, Little Rock, the Eisenhower administration found it necessary to use Army paratroopers (September 1958). In defiance of the Supreme Court ruling against the "separate but equal doctrine" Faubus closed four high schools in Little Rock and, in a move to reopen them on a segregated basis as private but state-financed institutions,

granted a charter to the Little Rock Private School Corporation. A year later his closing of the schools was declared unconstitutional.

Favela Brazilian slum.

Higuera Village where, after his capture by Bolivian government troops, Che Guevara was murdered.

Hostos y Bonilla, Puerto Rican Patriot, a pamphleteer, newspaper publisher,
Eugenio María political agitator, teacher, and literary scholar. Born in
1839-1903 Mayagüez, Puerto Rico, he was deeply involved in the struggle to free the Spanish Antilles from their colonialist masters and advocated a union of Cuba, Puerto Rico, and Santo Domingo. Forced into exile, he resided on various occasions in Spain, France, the United States, and a number of Latin-American countries. When the United States took over in Puerto Rico where the Spaniards left off, Hostos left his homeland for Santo Domingo rather than be directly subject to the new imperialism. He died there a short time later. Besides numerous articles, speeches, and booklets, his more celebrated writing include *La peregrinación de Bayoan* (1872), a novel, and *Moral Social* (1888).

Inti, Pablito, el Chino Members of the Bolivian guerrilla band led by Ernesto
and Aniceto Che Guevara and mentioned in his *Bolivian Diaries*.

Johnson, John Arthur First black man to hold the World Heavyweight Boxing
"Jack" Championship, which he won decisively by knocking out
1878-1946 Tommy Burns on Christmas Day in Sydney in 1908. One by one Johnson defeated each "White Hope" who challenged him, and earned an unprecedented $600,000 as a champion. He lost the title to Jess Willard in 1915 in Havana. His breaking of Boxing's color bar, somewhat flamboyant life-style, and associations with white women made him a controversial figure. While still champion he was the victim of a trumped-up Mann Act conviction and fled to Europe to avoid prosecution. After losing his title, he surrendered to United States Marshals and served the sentence. Before retiring he had a few more minor professional fights and performed occasionally in carnivals and vaudeville. When he died in Raleigh, North Carolina, he was penniless and largely forgotten.

| Kenskoff | A medium-sized town and mountain resort on the Massif de la Selle, Department d'Ouest. It is six miles south-south-east of Port-au-Prince and has an altitude of 4,400 feet above sea level. |

Kid Chocolate

Ring name of Eligio Sardiñas, born in Havana, 1910. He had won 100 amateur fights (86 by knockout) before his eighteenth birthday. He left Cuba for New York and fought his first fight in the Madison Square Garden late in 1928. When he retired some ten years later, Sardiñas held both the Featherweight and Junior Lightweight championships. In the United States he fought 122 times winning 109, 42 by knockout. He became quite popular in New York and was something of a national hero at home. "Small Ode to a Black Cuban Boxer" (p. 53) was written for Sardiñas and originally entitled "Small Ode for Kid Chocolate." Guillén himself has called it "my first *black* poem."

Kikuyu

A Bantu-speaking tribe in the highland area of the south-central part of Kenya. Counting their dozen or so sub-groups, they number approximately 1,000,000 and comprise the largest tribal group in the country. Their lands lie adjacent to European-settled areas and to the city of Nairobi.

Langford, Sam

The so-called "Boston Tar Baby," he was one of the greatest prizefighters of all time. Despite his obvious talents he was prevented from ever fighting in a title bout because of the unwritten law which, especially after Jack Johnson (q.v.), would not allow Negroes to fight whites. He made over $200,000 in the ring, with only 23 losses (3 by knockout) in 250 fights and, in 1956, was finally elected to Boxing's Hall of Fame, Old Timers Division. Like Jack Johnson, and indeed most black pugilists of the day, he was penniless and nearly forgotten in his last years. By 1935 he was a blind derelict in Harlem who, with the assistance of a sports writer who managed to establish a fund for him, received $1.65 a day for the remainder of his life.

La Citadelle

One of the wonders of the Western Hemisphere, La Citadelle La Ferrière stands majestically on the summit of Bonnet-a-l'Evêque at 2,800 feet in Haiti's central mountain range. It was constructed by Henri Christophe (q.v.)

as a castle-fortress in the event of a French invasion. The invasion never materialized and La Citadelle, its walls in some places 140 feet high and 30 feet thick, was never occupied.

LeClerc, Charles Victor
Emmanuel
1772-1802

Born in Pontoise, France, brother-in-law of Napoleon Bonaparte, he entered the army as a cavalryman in 1791 and six years later was a Brigadier General. He was Napoleon's Adjutant during the Italian campaign (1796), served in the Egyptian campaign (1798) and, now a General of Division, played a major role in the overthrow of the Directory (1799). In 1801 he took charge of the 34,000 men dispatched to retake San Domingue from L'Ouverture (q.v.). He died late the following year at La Tortue of yellow fever, leaving Rochambeau (q.v.) in charge of a badly failing campaign. Besides the countless Blacks who were dead or wounded, 24,000 of LeClerc's men had died, 8,000 were incapacitated by illness or wounds, and the remaining 2,000 were mostly exhausted and spiritless. Before his death LeClerc, whose secret orders from Bonaparte included the restoration of slavery, confessed this racist venture was not only a crime unworthy of civilized men, but also a horrible failure.

Leopoldina

A Brazilian village and railroad station in the state of and about ninety miles northwest of Rio de Janeiro.

Las Vegas

A reference to the presence of United States military testing and proving grounds in the deserts of Nevada and other western states.

L'Ouverture, Toussaint
1745-1803

A slave to the age of forty-five, he became the most powerful and diplomatically adept of the several leaders of the slave insurrection begun in 1791. He learned from all those—white or black—with whom he came in contact and, by imposing a rigid discipline among his followers, built an army of ex-slaves that allowed him to assume complete power in San Domingue and to keep the various European powers from invading successfully and reimposing slavery. Despite his virtual declaration of independence in the constitution of 1801, he was reluctant to sever completely the island's, now merely formal, ties to France. Finally duped and kidnapped by Napoleon's agents, he was deported to France where, imprisoned and denied any aid or medical care, he died an ignominious death.

Maceo, Antonio
1848-1896

A brilliant leader in the struggles for Cuban independence from Spain, he stands with Martí (q.v.) and Che Guevara as one of that country's most revered patriots. Praised for his bravery, tenacity and cleverness in battle even by Spanish historians, between 1868-78 he rose to the rank of Major General and commanded insurgent forces in Oriente province. When a temporary truce was declared in 1878 he fled to Jamaica. From there he passed to Honduras and with the rank of General, commanded anti-colonialist forces in Puerto Cortés province. From then until his definitive return to the island he was active (at times from abroad, at times in Cuba) in every aspect of the Cuban independence movement. When the Spaniards were threatened anew by serious revolutionary outbreaks (1895) Maceo returned secretly to Cuba and led a growing number of troops in a triumphant sweep of the island. After distinguishing himself further in the famous battle of Peralejo (q.v.) he fell in a minor engagement near Havana. Since he was black, his memory is particularly cherished by South Americans of that color. His fame has also spread to the north where occasionally one encounters a Black bearing the given name Maceo. A notable example of this is the first son of Eldridge and Katheline Cleaver, born a few years ago in Cuba.

Macheteros

Literally, machete-man, cane cutters. It is also used to refer to Cuban rebels during the Ten-Years War (1868-78) who, for lack of weapons, usually fought with machetes.

Magdalena, the

A large river, Colombia's principal trade artery, which empties into the sea near the city of Baranquilla. The main crops of its fertile valley are sugar, cotton, tobacco, coffee, and bananas.

Magoon, Charles Edward
1861-1920

Born in Minnesota, he studied at the University of Nebraska and was admitted to the bar in 1882. His involvement in colonial questions began with an appointment to the War Department's Bureau of Insular Affairs in 1899. There, with the title of Law Officer, Magoon specialized in Puerto Rico, Cuba, and the Philippines. In 1904-05, as General Counsel to the Isthmian Canal Commission, he prepared laws for the administration of the Panama Canal Zone. In 1905-06 Magoon was Governor of the Canal Zone and United States Minister to Panama. In 1906 he was appointed Provisional Governor of Cuba, a post he held for three years. He is remembered to this day on the island for faithfully perpetuating the system of graft and corruption he had inherited. Under his administration the governor's office became primarily the source and disseminator of patronage. His book, *The Law of Civil Government in Territory Subject to Military Occupation (1902),* outlines his ideas on the administration of imperialism's spoils.

Martí, Jose
1853-1895

Gifted stylist, sensitive poet, devoted journalist, and respected diplomat, he is credited with having done more than any other single person in the furtherance of Cuba's independence from Spain, a cause to which he dedicated himself from the age of sixteen. Twice exiled from Cuba, he studied in Spain, was professor of Law at the University of Guatemala, and founded the Cuban Revolutionary Party. He lived for a long time in New York where he acted as consul to the United States of America from Paraguay, Uruguay, and Argentina. At the age of forty-two he led a group of armed revolutionaries from the United States to Cuba, disembarked secretly, and joined the rebel forces of General Máximo Gómez. A short time later he was killed in battle near Dos Ríos.

Martinsville

A reference to the legal murder of six Negro youths and an older Negro man—the Martinsville (Va.) Seven—for the alleged rape of a local white store manager's wife in 1949. Their arrest and subsequent conviction, by an *all-white* jury, in an atmosphere marked by racist hysteria, produced a wave of nationwide and international protest. Among those protesting, author Howard Fast was moved to address an open letter to fellow writers John Steinbeck, Arthur Miller, Erskine Caldwell, Ernest Hemingway, Lillian Hellman, Irwin Shaw, Vincent Sheean, Budd Schulberg, Archibald MacLeish, Carl Sandburg, Upton Sinclair and John Hersey, which read in part: "I address myself to you not with a plea—the time for pleading is done with—but with a solemn warning that unless you raise your voices to protest this unspeakable thing that is happening here in America [the murder of Black men and women by legal means], your own walls of comfort and security will crumble away in the not too distant future, and the price you will pay will be no less than the price Hitler exacted from the intellectuals of Germany. Nothing except a great voice

of wrath and horror can atone for the crime of your silence." Appeals to the Supreme Court were refused and,
in 1951, the several defendents—Joe Henry Hampton,
Howard Hairston, James Hairston, Frank Hairston, Booker
Millner, John Taylor, and Francis Grayson—were duly
executed in the electric chair.

Muñoz Marín, Luis
1898-

After the United States Congress agreed to allow the people of Puerto Rico to choose their own Chief Executive, he
was elected Governor in 1948, 1952, 1956, and 1960. He
spent much of his youth on the mainland, graduated from
Georgetown University, and from 1916 to 1918 was Secretary to the Puerto Rican Commissioner to the Congress.
He belonged to both the Socialist and Liberal Parties. An
early advocate of Puerto Rican independence and Latin
American unity, he underwent a change of outlook late in
the 1930's; he was expelled from the Liberal Party (1937),
founded the Popular Democratic Party (1938), and became a close ally of those who believed Puerto Rico was
not "ready" for real independence from the United States
of America. During his years as President of the Senate
(1941-48) he cooperated fully with the United States-ap-
pointed governor and worked tirelessly to make the latter's
policies a success there. In a word, Muñoz Marín has had
more to do than any other Puerto Rican with the present
state of affairs in Puerto Rico and its relationship with the
United States. In 1963 he was awarded the Presidential
Medal of Freedom by Lyndon B. Johnson.

O'Donnell, Leopoldo
1808-1867

Captain-General of Cuba (1843-1848), he is famous for
his involvement in the slave trade, his repressive policies
in favor of the plantocracy, and for his implacable handling
of the aborted slave insurrection *La conspiración de la
escalera* (1844). The repression which followed this con-
spiracy of the ladder—so called because blacks arrested for
plotting were tied to ladders and whipped until they confessed or died—claimed, among its more notable victims,
the mulatto poet "Plácido," Gabriel de la Concepción
Váldés.

Otero Silva, Miguel
1908-

Venezuelan novelist, his works include *Casas Muertes*
(1955) and *Fiebre* (1939), a novel about the student opposition to the dictator Gómez.

Peralejo	A small region situated between the town of Bayamo and the Buey River in Cuba's Oriente Province. It is the site of one of the most famous battles in the wars for independence from Spain. There, on July 15, 1895, Spanish troops commanded by General Martínez Campos were badly defeated by a large number of insurgents under Antonio Maceo (q.v.). As a result the rebels gained definitive control of that region, insurgent Quintín Banderas assumed administrative authority there, and a major psychological defeat was suffered by the "old and beaten lion."
Pernambuco	From Indian words *pera nambuco* meaning perforated rock, a Brazilian State located on the Atlantic Ocean in the northeastern part of the country. Its capital, Recife, is also called Pernambuco. Once the seat of the *quilombo,* the Republic founded by escaped slaves in 1630, the area's principal wealth is in agriculture, especially sugar, cotton, and tobacco.
Pétionville	Also Pétion-ville, this small city is an exclusive residential suburb and very chic resort area three and a half miles east-southeast of Port-au-Prince on the north hills of the Massif de la Selle, Department d'Ouest. It is named for Anne-Alexandre Sabrès Pétion (1770-1818), the son of a free black woman, Ursule Pétion, and a wealthy French colonist, Pascal Sabrès. Because of his strongly Negroid features, the father refused to recognize him; hence the use of the maternal surname. After graduation from a military academy in Paris, he returned to Haiti as an officer in the French army (1791) and was subsequently embroiled in the tragic and highly complicated Black-White-Mulatto warfare which tore the island apart for two decades. At one time or another he fought with the forces of everyone from Dessalines (q.v.) to LeClerc (q.v.). When Christophe (q.v.) assumed the presidency after Dessalines' death, the south and west provinces preferred Pétion and chose him President (1807). His section of the island, mostly mulatto, and that of Christophe battled constantly. In 1815 Pétion was elected president for life with the power to name his successor. Soon thereafter the problems of state began to take a heavy toll on his mental energies; he fell into a state of hypochondria and melancholy and, about a week before his forty-eighth birthday, he died.

Platt Amendment, the	In 1901 Senator Orville H. Platt of Connecticut proposed an amendment to the United States Army appropriations bill, based on the formulations of War Secretary Elihu Root, which set forth the conditions under which the United States would end its military occupation of Cuba. Two of its most significant provisions were the right to intervene at any time should Cuba's "independence" be threatened, and to build a naval base somewhere on the island. The amendment, written into Cuba's constitution and recognized via a special treaty between the two countries, virtually nullified that document. In 1934, as part of the so-called Good Neighbor Policy, a new treaty was signed by which the United States relinquished all the original treaty afforded them except the naval base at Guantanamo, which remains a bone of contention.
Pont-Rouge	A small district on the outskirts of Port-au-Prince where disloyal officials fell upon Dessalines (q.v.), murdered him, then mutilated and pillaged his body. Proof of the fear and respect he inspired is the fact that only after shooting his horse from under him did the assassins dare to approach with pistols and sabres as he lay pinned with a broken leg. Pont-Rouge is also the name of the small bridge onto which the emperor rode to survey the situation just before he was attacked.
Rochambeau, Donatien Marie Joseph de Vimeur, Vicomte de 1750-1813	Lieutenant General who commanded the French auxiliaries in the American war for independence and took part in George Washington's defeat of Cornwallis at Yorktown in 1781. Young Rochambeau, on taking command of the LeClerc (q.v.) expedition, was sent approximately 20,000 reinforcements from France, and soon many of the soldiers already there began to recover from the fever. The French then set about a cruel war of sadistic torture and genocide. Blacks were drowned, hanged, dismembered, burned, and burned alive. People were forced to watch while members of their families were killed. Like the Spaniards in Cuba and the English in Jamaica, Rochambeau used a special breed of bloodhound to hunt and kill Blacks. He had a small amphitheatre constructed and, while gaily-dressed spectators watched, these dogs were allowed to devour alive black prisoners. But his efforts were in vain; he was driven out by Dessalines (q.v.) in 1803 and taken prisoner by the English Navy less than two

weeks later. He remained in custody until 1811 when he was exchanged. Two years later he was killed in the Battle of Leipzig.

Sandino, César Augusto
1893-1934

A most exemplary Nicaraguan patriot, this son of a small farmer came to national prominence in 1926 as a leader in the struggle to support Vice-President Juan Bautista Sacasa's claim to the Presidency. When the United States intervened in 1927 to assure "peace" Sandino and his followers responded with a highly successful guerrilla-type operation against the imperialist invaders. They were able to outwit repeatedly both United States Marines and the Nicaraguan National Guard, gaining support of the country's masses and a good deal of sympathy abroad. Only when the Marines were forced to depart in 1933 and Sacasa was inaugurated did Sandino agree to lay down his arms. Early the following year he was murdered by members of the National Guard after dining one evening with President Sacasa. The "official" explanation is that these men were wary of Sandino's potential political power and angry at the soft treatment the former "outlaw" had received. The contemporary Nicaraguan poet Ernesto Cardenal recalls the situation in his poem "Zero Hour."

Stroessner, Alfredo
General
1912-

Dictator of Paraguay, a symbol of traditional militarism and caudillismo in Latin America. The son of a brewer of German extraction, he joined the army at sixteen, became a cadet at the military school, and later earned himself a reputation and a commission during the Chaco War of the early thirties between his country and Bolivia. In 1950, under the Presidency of Dr. Federico Chávez, Stroessner became Chief of the Armed Forces. From his new post he engineered the coup that ended Chávez' reign in 1954 and, running unopposed, was "elected" President for the next four years. He began his regime by increasing the repression of all opposition and with his "Law for the Defense of Democracy" (1955) extended his presidential prerogatives to include a nonconsultative power to declare national emergencies, state supervision, regulation and organization of all public groups as well as expedient limitation of all civil liberties. Stroessner has managed to keep himself in power by skillful alliances with the conservative Colorado Party, his control of the Armed Forces and, of course, United States aid sent on the premise that "a sure anti-Communist, no matter how despicable, is better than a reformer, no matter how honest, who might turn against us."

Sun Yat-Sen
1866-1925

Known also as Sun Wen, and Chung Shan. A graduate of English schools and Hong Kong College of Medicine (1892), his democratic revolutionary activities against the Manchu (Ch'ing) Dynasty forced him into exile in 1895. From then until the fall of the monarchy in 1911 he was the principal organizer of worldwide support in behalf of Republican interests in his country. He founded the T'ung Meng Hui (Revolutionary Alliance), the Kuo-Ming-T'ang (Nationalist Party), and was the first President of the Republic. He was forced to share power with Yuan Shih K'ai, a powerful militarist from the north with a strong well-trained army and a great deal of material aid from Western banking interests; when this arrangement became impossible he formed a separate democratic nationalist government (1921) in Canton. He died without ever seeing his country united. In his struggle against northern warlords during the final years of his life, he worked closely with the Chinese Communists and advocated more intimate ties between China and the Soviet Union. His widow (Ch'ing Ling Soon), the sister of Mme. Chiang Kai-Shek and of United States-educated banker T.V. Soon, became a prominent official in the People's Government after World War II. Sun Yat-Sun's Principal writings are *Memories of a Chinese Revolutionary* (1927), *The Three Principles of the People* (1927), and *Outlines of National Reconstruction* (1929).

Taft, William Howard
1857-1930

Besides serving as the twenty-seventh President of the United States, he was Solicitor General, Head of the Philippine Commission, First Civil Governor of the Philippines, Secretary of War, Professor of Law at both Cincinnati Law School and Yale, and Chief Justice of The United States Supreme Court from 1921 to his death. As Secretary of War he was sent to Cuba in 1906 to reestablish United States authority and restore "order" in the wake of the hotly contested general elections. He brought with him some 2,000 Marines and about 5,600 other military personnel. After serving briefly as Provisional Governor, Taft departed, leaving Magoon (q.v.) in control.

| Tarapacá | A state with a capital of the same name, in Chile which lies between the Andes and the Pacific Ocean and borders Peru and Bolivia. It contains immense deposits of easily exploitable nitrate of soda which are transported from the desert to the coast by railroad. |

| Till, Emmett 1941-1955 | The case to which this poem refers is the so-called "Wolf-whistle" murder. In the summer of 1955 the youth, while visiting relatives in Money, Mississippi, is said to have whistled in appreciation at the wife of a local white store-owner. According to one of the murderers, who later related the story to a church deacon in a fit of drunken-ness, the boy was kidnapped from his grandparents' house at gunpoint, beaten severely, and shot to death. The body was tied to the wheel of an old cotton gin and thrown into a river. Police are said to have known about the atrocity, but in keeping with unwritten law in that part of the coun-try (no penalty for Negro deaths) an investigation was not undertaken. Only due to the efforts of Dr. T. R. M. Howard, a local black physician, were northern journalists made aware of the crime, an inquiry begun, and two men brought to trial. In spite of the black witnesses who testi-fied (others either disappeared or were afraid to speak in court), the accused went free. Both Dr. Howard and Mandy Bradley, one of the witnesses, were harassed and threat-ened to the point of having to leave the state. The body of Emmett Till, just as it had been dredged from the river, was shipped in a cheap pine box to Chicago to a funeral home where it was claimed by the victim's mother. This crime took place just one year after a Supreme Court decision outlawed racial segregation in Public Schools, and less than a year before the black boycott which desegregated public bus service in Montgomery, Alabama. Ten years later Malcolm X was killed in New York by unknown persons; twelve years later Martin Luther King was slain; fifteen years later Black Panther Fred Hampton was shot to death in his sleep by Chicago police officers; and sixteen years later Soledad brother George Jackson was shot by prison guards at San Quentin. |

| Tocopilla | An important shipping port, located in the state of Anto-fagasta, for the nitrate industry of Chile. The area also yields large amounts of iodine and copper. See also Pablo |

Neruda's "Cristóbal Miranda: Palero-Tocopilla" collected in the "La tierra se llama Juan," Section IV of *Canto General.*

Trujillo, Rafael Leonidas
1891-1961

Dictator of the Dominican Republic from 1930 until his death. He originally seized power in a revolt against President Horacio Vásquez and was "elected" a few months later. His official terms in office were 1930-38 and 1942-52. He was able to maintain his position via control of the country's armed forces, ruthless suppression of dissent, almost total curtailment of civil liberties and, of course, massive quantities of United States military and economic aid.

Turquino

El Turquino, located to the south of Bayamo in Oriente province, is the highest peak in the Sierra Maestra and the culminating point in the orographic system of the Antilles.

Veracruz

Originally *La Villa Rica de la Vera Cruz* (Rich town of the True Cross), this port city approximately 200 air miles east of Mexico City in the state of the same name was built by Hernando Córtez in 1519 as a base for the conquest of Mexico. The incident to which Guillén refers has roots in President Woodrow Wilson's antipathy toward the policies of Victoriano Huerta, Provisional President of Mexico. On April 19, 1914, a group of sailors from the *U.S.S. Dolphin* were detained briefly for disorderly conduct by Mexican Police in Tampico. Greatly incensed, United States authorities demanded, among other things, that the American Flag on the *Dolphin* be granted a twenty-one gun salute by way of apology. When the Mexicans refused, Wilson sent a war fleet to the gulf and requested from congress permission to intervene in Mexico. While they were debating the issue, the German merchant ship *Ypiranga* entered the Gulf with munitions for Huerta. To prevent the munitions from reaching Huerta, Wilson issued an Executive Order to occupy Veracruz. In the intensive shelling and combat which ensued over 200 Mexican soldiers were killed. The city was occupied until November of that year. Even Huerta's Mexican opponents denounced this bold and cruel act of imperialism, but the President was forced to resign and a regime more to Wilson's liking did come to power.

Walker, William 1824-60	A lawyer, physician, editor, and journalist, he is best known as the most active and cruel of nineteenth-century filibusters. In 1853 he commanded an expedition which landed in La Paz, Lower California; he proclaimed it an independent state and himself president. Hostile Mexican and uncooperative United States authorities caused the mission to fail. Walker stood trial in San Francisco for violation of neutrality laws but was easily acquitted by a sympathetic jury. Three years later with help from the Accessory Transit Company (American), he seized and proclaimed himself president of Nicaragua. Supported by influencial southerners in Government and business, he repealed a Nicaraguan decree which had abolished slavery, and went about making Central America safe for the expansion of southern economic interests. Later he was deposed for siding with the Accessory Transit Company against the interests of Cornelius Vanderbilt in that part of the world. While attempting to return to Nicaragua by way of Honduras, Walker was captured by British authorities and turned over to the Hondurans who promptly put him before a firing squad.
Weyler, General Valeriano, Marqués de Tenerife 1838-1930	Commander of Spanish forces during Cuban revolutionary war of 1895, he followed a policy of complete ruthlessness during his campaign. He is particularly remembered for his policy of moving the Cuban population into compounds, *reconcentrados,* in order to prevent their helping the rebel forces.
Wills, Harry	A black prizefighter and one of the leading pugilists of the twenties in the United States. His continual challenges of Jack Dempsey were rebuffed and eventually led to the latter's being tagged "Champion of the White Folks." Wills, like Langford (q.v.), whom he fought twenty-two times, and Jack Johnson (q.v.) before him was a victim of Boxing's color bar. When in 1922, Dempsey, to the disbelief of white commentators, agreed to meet Wills it seemed that another test of white supremacy reminiscent of the Johnson-Tommy Burns bout was in the offing. Dempsey, however, never made good his promise.
Wood, Leonard 1860-1927	An American military man, physician, and colonial administrator, he entered the army by way of the medical corps after receiving an M.D. from Harvard in 1884. Two

years later he won the Medal of Honor for his part as a leader of men and doctor in a brutal campaign to suppress the Apache Chief Geronimo. As White House Physician to William McKinley he helped his close friend, Assistant Secretary of the Navy Theodore Roosevelt, to declare war on Spain in 1898. With the rank of Colonel he helped Roosevelt recruit and commanded the United States Volunteer Cavalry (Rough Riders) which invaded Cuba. After receiving a field promotion to Brigadier General and with the fall of Santiago, he was made Governor of Oriente Province. Later in 1899, with the rank of Major General, he was appointed Governor of Cuba; he held the position until 1902. He was subsequently assigned to the Philippines where he served for a time as governor of Moro province and became famous for his ruthless measures against anti-American forces. From 1906-08, now a General in the regular Army, Wood commanded the United States Philippine Division. Fifteen years later he was appointed Governor General of the Philippines and was successful in smashing the growing self-government movement there. His excessive personal ambitions alienated him from civilian officials, and he did not see action in World War I. He was nearly the Republican candidate for President in 1920 and throughout his life Wood was a loud, tireless, and somewhat popular advocate of militarism and imperialism. In his obituary, the *New York Times* referred to him as "America's Proconsul."

**Wu Sang-Kuei, General
1612-1678**

Feudal warlord of the Ch'ing period and founder of kingdom of Chou (1673-81). Designated "Earl Who Pacifies the West," in 1644 he was ordered to Peking to repel an attack by Li Tzu-Ch'eng. He delayed and, on hearing of the fall of the city, turned back to Shanhaikan where, popular belief has it he went to surrender to Li Tzu-Ch'eng who held his father hostage. He eventually opposed Li Tzu-Ch'eng, however, and built himself an army of followers so powerful they gave him control of Yunnan, Kweichow, Hunnan, Szechwan, Shensi, and Kansu and proved a severe burden on the royal treasury. Having served the cause of the Manchus for approximately thirty years, he revolted in 1673 when it seemed certain that Peking favored abolition of the feudatories system. Murdering all officials who opposed him and assuming control of the country's armies, he established his Chou

Dynasty and, a year later, by declaring war on the Manchu began the so-called "War of the Three Feudatories" (Besides Wu Sang-Kuei's there were those of Keng Ching-Chung and Shang Chin-Hsin). In 1678 he declared himself emperor of Chou and five months later died of dysentery. The death of his son, Wu Ying-Hsiung, in 1681 ended the rebellion and the dynasty that began with it.

Zulia

A state in northwest Venezuela whose capital is the large industrial city of Maracaibo. Its territory almost entirely encircles Lake Maracaibo. It is the center of Venezuela's oil industry and contains one of the world's richest deposits of crude petroleum.

Note on Sources

The poems included in this anthology were taken from the various volumes of Guillén's work, as herewith indicated:

Motivos de son 1930
My Little Woman

Sóngoro consongo 1931
Arrival
Small ode to a Black
  Cuban Boxer

West Indies, Ltd. 1934
Words in the Tropics
Ballad of the Two Gandfathers
Heat

**Cantos para soldados y
  sones para turistas** 1937
Execution

El son entero 1947
A son for Antillian
  Children

**La paloma de vuelo
  popular** 1958
Sports
Neighborhood house
Exile
Song for Puerto Rico
Little Rock
Rivers
Short Grotesque Litany
  on The Death of
  Senator McCarthy
Bars
5 Chinese Songs
Mau-Maus
Cities
Carioca Song
Paul Éluard
Little Ballad of Plovdiv

Sputnik 57

Elegías 1958 (complete)
Cuban Elegy
My Last Name
Elegy for Emmett Till
Elegy for Jacques Roumain
Elegy for Camagüey
Elegy for Jesús Menéndez

Tengo 1964
Bonsal
The Flowers Grow High
Far Off
Soviet Union
Whatever Time is past
  was Worst
Thus Sings a Mockingbird
  in El Turquino
Sell Me?
I came on a slave ship
Brazil-Copacabana
Land in the Sierra and
  The Plain
A Black Man Sings in
  New York City
Wu Sang-Kuei
In The Winter in París

Poemas de amor 1964
Ovenstone
Ana María

Poemas para el Che 196?
Guitar in Mourning Major
Sunday Reading

La rueda dentada
  (unpublished)
The Cosmonaut
What Color?
Ancestry

Angela Davis
  (Unpublished)